The Beautiful You

A Self-Care Toolkit Guide

By Balanced Flame

Cover Illustration by Ellis Lewis-Dragstra

Instagram Ellis_L.D

Paperback ISBN: 978-1-0685809-0-1

Hardback ISBN: 978-1-0685809-1-8

Ebook ISBN: 978-1-0685809-2-5

For

The Beautiful You

Contents

Introduction

Hello, beautiful you. Take a deep breath in and out. Know you are seen. Every part of you is welcome—the weird, the wacky, the wounded, the wonderful, the wild, the wise, the wishful. You and I are a magical blend of it all, yet we are also more than any description. All these parts come together to create the beautiful you, and the beautiful me. Beneath it all lies our radiant, infinite soul, witnessing and embracing every experience, linking us to a meaning beyond this lifetime.

***

Welcome to this little book of expressions from me, 'Balanced Flame,' the name I have adopted to share my thoughts and practices with you; my deep introversion now flipping 180 Degrees to complete extroversion!

The name Balanced Flame is a reminder to myself of what I am striving for every day. I feel that an aim in life is to achieve the perfect balance in all that we do. Balance is what keeps us healthy, strong, and happy. It is to be the healer and the warrior. To embrace our shadow as well as our light. To spend equal time in work, play and self-care.

Each of us has a light within us, with fire being the element of our heart. This flame is within each of us, and we must tend to it and expand it; this is our duty. This flame, this light, is what can lift us into positive and beautiful life experiences for ourselves and those around us as we radiate at the vibration of love.

Of course, we are human and will experience less pleasant emotions and circumstances; that is part of the journey.

We learn to embrace the challenges. Really feel into the depths of the pain, the anger, the despair.

Then we learn to let go; we do not need to carry them with us forever, especially when our outer circumstances change and no longer reflect this.

We can stay present to life as it is happening now; we do not need to hold on to negative emotions or experiences of the past. And holding grudges is never beneficial. The more forgiveness and understanding we practice, the happier we will be, understanding that everyone is on their own journey, and many things are not personal, so we do not need to take them as such.

We can choose to be a warrior and grow and transform from pain, instead of slipping into victim mentality. Of course, life circumstances impact this, and some people are dealt a much more challenging hand than others, requiring greater strength to overcome the challenge.

If this is you, just know that Great Spirit believes you have the inner strength to overcome challenges that come your way. Do not be afraid to ask Spirit for help and guidance. Remember this current life is just one chapter of our souls' experience; each chapter has different challenges we must face, in order to strengthen our spirit.

Remember to work with your breath. Breathe into the Lower Dantian energy centre (point below belly button- breathe into your belly). Hold your energy in this focus point to feel calm and balanced. Breathe out your mouth, letting go of all that does not serve you.

Try to train your subconscious breath to be 'belly breathing', not chest breathing. As babies we breathe into our bellies, yet as we get older and more stressed and anxious due to life circumstances, we resort to shallow chest breathing. This is less nourishing and regulating for our system.

Breathe deeply and fully, breathing in intentions of peace and breathing out any tension or pain. Our breath is our most constant system cleanser; the more we consciously work with it in this way, the more benefits for health and wellbeing it provides.

We need to also be mindful of what we consume: food, drinks, substances, body products, external negativity etc; and being aware of the impact things have on our physical, mental and emotional body. This ultimately impacts our spirit too. To be careful what we feed and fill our minds with, making conscious effort to have positive thought patterns and training our internal self-talk to be gentle, courageous, kind.

The world can beat us down, but in our internal world, we decide the vibe. I choose to be a best friend to myself rather than a worst enemy. We have this choice in every moment. Choose wisely, as remember you are the one who always has your back, who shows up for you every day. Look into your own eyes with wonder and admiration at your journey, your energy, your being. Be kind to you, give yourself love so you are full, then any other love you receive is a pleasant bonus.

I did not always have this mental state as my baseline. As light as my mind and energy can be, the flip side is the darkest of dark, a mental space I experienced through my teenage years and dip into when triggered by life's traumas. But I made it through and now have all my tools to support me out of those dark places. This book is to share my journey of finding 'the beautiful me' within me, in the wish that it will support you in finding and connecting with 'the beautiful you', within you.

Life is all about testing our perseverance to rise up again after every challenge and our response to what happens. Sometimes the rise may take longer than others. Have faith in ourselves and our strength. I believe in me and I believe in you.

Remember to zoom out your perspective and marvel at the miracle of everything, aware that we are part of something much bigger than ourselves. On a beautiful planet that is rotating a huge ball of fire, just one part of the great omniverse we are within. Oh the miracle of it all.

Inspiration Behind This Book

I initially wrote these poems as personal expressions—they helped me to process and express what was going on in my mind and make sense of situations, increase my understanding, process difficult events and expand ideas on life, the universe, consciousness and explore different 'rabbit holes' of thought trains. Writing is a great tool for me.

I shared some poems with family and friends who told me my poems made them feel good and that I could share them wider, as they may help others too. Hence the writing of this book!

I have included some key insights into my journey at the beginning of the book and between some of the poems (and some raw emotional journalling throughout, as life kept happening as I was putting this book together!), as I wish to be open and give you, the reader, some understanding to the life stage or experiences from which each poem was written, offering an insight into my perfectly imperfect character, as a transparent human experience. I express my shadow as well as my light, as I am both. I do not disclose all of my experiences, as that would call for a series haha but offer deep snapshots and shares into parts of my journey.

After feeling close to death in a variety of ways, I have the understanding that while we are here, it can serve our highest good to be brave, take risks and just go for it (following gut feeling as a compass). I feel that life is to be lived and expressed, and who knows who may benefit from what we put out into the world. Even if just one person benefits positively, then it is worth it. If this is resonating with you in some way, I encourage you to be brave, follow your dreams, and just do it.

Life is impermanent and if I die tomorrow, I want to feel I really lived. Living each day like it is our last helps us to be present, courageous, grateful and make each moment sacred.

What You Will Find Here

This is a book of poems with added insights into some of my life experiences and encounters which inspired me to write. It is a self-care toolkit guide as it includes techniques and ideas which support good health and well-being, which I have tried and implemented on my own healing journey. You may wish to extract parts that resonate with you and use them as ideas or techniques to support your health and wellbeing too. Some concepts may repeat, conveying the importance of the message.

The poems have a spiritual element and contain expressions of spirituality, grief, darkness and light, perspectives, connection, heavy emotions, positive emotions, ideas, life events and a miscellaneous category. My intention with deciding to share my poems is to offer hope and perhaps unconsidered perspectives to help you get through challenges you are facing, whether that be grief or any other trauma, or even just to give you 'food for thought' on this life adventure we are all experiencing. You may find some things relatable to your own experience and be reminded that you are not alone.

My brothers and sisters of the Earth, we stand together, holding hands, side by side. I love you. The world needs us to tune into our frequency of love.

Self-Care Toolkit

At the end I have provided a section called 'Self-Care Toolkit' which gives some guidance and pointers for things you can try. These are things that have helped me greatly, influencing my health and well-being and energy and are in my own 'Self-care toolkit'. Some are mentioned throughout the book, however at the end is where you will find them all in one place for easier reference, if you feel drawn to try anything yourself. On the last page of this book is a space for you to build and create your own personal self-care toolkit.

You may be new to this concept, or you may already have different practices that bring you good health and wellbeing. Always listen to your body and see what practices make your heart lift and your energy expand.

Remember we cannot be fully flourishing all the time, be gentle with yourself wherever you are at and remember healing is not a linear journey. We all experience setbacks and new challenges.

It requires consistent effort and intention to maintain good health and wellbeing and doing this when in good health is also important, as prevention is better than cure.

Personal Message to You

This book has found its way to you for a reason…I send you love, healing and good vibes now, and for the rest of your journey.

May you live a life of adventure, love, trust and joy.

May you find your inner strength to overcome all challenges which come your way and may you extract all the learnings necessary for your soul growth.

May your inner voice always be gentle.

Remember you are so powerful! Ride the flow, remember without the dark times there is no light, and remember no one is perfect, we each have a shadow which is ours to embrace in love. We are all perfectly imperfect, the balance of Yin and Yang within us. To accept and hold them both in a warm loving embrace is to become whole again.

To also accept this same fact for others- we should not expect anyone to be perfect, as that is impossible here. Everyone has strengths and flaws and we can love and accept all of them.

A big learning for me is that through pain and trauma, we can always choose to channel our energy into creative endeavours and create something beautiful and heal in the process.

On Truth

It is okay if you do not understand or agree with some of the concepts mentioned. I am not declaring them as everyone's truth, only my truth, which was true to me at the time I wrote it. We each can only determine real 'truth' through our own experience.

Remember, everyone lives in a different reality, shaped by their experiences, environment, personality, thought patterns and of course perspective. Each of us holding a unique wealth of experiences and challenges overcome, in addition to a set of beliefs which give our lives meaning. If these beliefs are of good intention and create positive and trusting feelings, the details and differences are not important. Every individual has a story to tell.

"Truth is an expression of an individual's reality at a certain time."

— My Super Mum

Remember, we are each our own greatest teacher, and all true masters will guide you to find the answers that are already within yourself. Always let yourself—your heart, your gut and your intuition be your ultimate guide.

Final Invitation

I invite you to explore this book and take it as suggestions and ideas for you to consider, supporting you on your journey finding your own inner truth and to develop your own self-care toolkit. Exploring the mysteries of life is also the invitation to accept that we will never really know for sure. We can formulate our own belief systems and understandings but there are many things which only the creator knows the answer to. Once we accept that uncertainty, we can carve our own meaning through experiences and transformations. There is always more to be learned. Just don't forget to have fun and enjoyment along the way. We don't need to know the answers to everything.

We just need to BE.

We are all students and we are all teachers. The learning never ends as there is always more to discover. I am learning every day.

Find your passions, follow your dreams, be kind to those you meet on your path. Connect with many, but attach to none. Life is about connection, not attachment. You are already whole and complete. Be fulfilled within you. The Beautiful You that you are, and that you strive to be.

So, welcome to my inner universe. Please leave shoes and judgements at the door; find freshly baked cookies and herbal teas on the side, and get comfortable.

Remember, "A mind is like a parachute- it only works when it's open".

Avatar

The first poem I want to share with you is 'Avatar'. In it, I mention 'Birth Charts' and I am referring to the stars and where they were positioned when we were born. It is Western Astrology- The Zodiac- Aries, Taurus, Gemini, Cancer, Leo, Virgo, Libra, Scorpio, Sagittarius, Capricorn, Aquarius and Pisces.

Many people have heard of 'Sun signs' but what is less well known is that actually where every planet in our solar system was when we were born, impacts different parts of our personality, e.g. Venus influences love and relationships, Mars influences primal energy, aggression and sex, Mercury influences our thinking and creativity and Saturn represents where our challenges in this life will be (I talk about this more in 'The Universe and Planets' poem later in this book).

This is why some people think that star signs are a hoax as they may not relate strongly to their Sun sign/ may relate to many signs, but there is an intricate and complex system to discover.

Some say the main three to know are our Sun sign, Moon sign and Rising/ Ascendant sign.

Your Rising/ Ascendant sign is how you are perceived by people in new situations. First impressions. It is also how you may be perceived when feeling anxious or uncomfortable in a situation. This is how 'acquaintances' may know you, especially if you have not opened up to them. (Some people you meet and get deep straight away, and they may see you as your sun or even moon sign, you know when you just 'click').

Your Sun sign is who your friends and family know you to be. Your circle. Those who you have let closer to you and get to know you. You have opened up more. It is how you show up in the world.

Your Moon sign is your soul self. The deep internal you, ruling your moods and emotions. It is who you know yourself to be. Those closest to you, in your inner, inner circle, those who you feel most comfortable around, will know this you too.

That is my understanding of it anyway and I imagine an image of a person with three rings inside the other. Like your inner and outer circles of connectivity to others.

Also, how we are feeling within ourselves (comfortable/ uncomfortable) can influence how we present too/ which sign is dominant in a given scenario. We feel most comfortable when we are surrounded by good willed, non-judgemental people who we feel safe enough consciously and subconsciously, to express our true self, who we know ourselves to be.

To find out your whole birth chart you need to know the time you were born, as well as the location and date. If you do not know your time you can state that on the chart and you can still find out most of it. You can find free charts online which can give you initial insight into which star sign the planets were in when you were born, then read for yourself and see what you think. For me it was pretty mind blowing and helped me understand my avatar a whole lot more.

Do not get too attached to this though as we are beyond this. We are an infinite soul living out another lifetime, in a different body to the last. We are that soul energy that fills a vessel, a temple. It is this body temple which changes each time we come to Earth and it is the birth chart which is like an instruction manual to each temple. This thought reminded me of a video game where you pick a character with different strengths and missions, but also weak points, and you 'spawn' into the game, inside this character. You are not the character, but you are the energy and intention coming through the character.

1. 'Avatar' 12.03.2021

Life is like a video game,
We are in our Avatar,
Our unique and special character.

We are born with imprints, like our personality,
Our skills, strengths and weaknesses,
Our star signs can give us clarity.

Our star sign birth chart is like our characters manual,
It can lay out our answers to the above,
And our life by day and annual.

The more we know our true self,
The more it will make sense,
Don't pass this off as nonsense,
Have a read,
then use your common sense!

Now, reading it first time, can be quite intense,
Find a quiet space, clear your mind, light some incense.

Set the intention to be open minded and don't take offence,

The stars know the whole you, more than you do,

TRUST- it's immense!

Remember though this is not YOU,

It is just the avatar you are playing,

It is what you are experiencing in this life,

To learn lessons, grow your soul…

Do you know what I'm saying?

Accept your character, love it all,

After all, you chose it,

and all the hardships you would face, big and small.

How do you feel knowing your soul knew you would not fail-

It knew you have the inner strength to always prevail.

So harness the gale,

Set sail!

Life does not have to be a jail…

Nor need to be boring and stale.

Jump down the rabbit hole, follow the trail.

Open your heart and mind…

Breathe in…Exhale.

Step back from your thoughts, use your senses, see what you unveil.

Magic and purpose is there… have good intentions, be kind, respect male and female.

See those around you beyond their avatar…
They are the same as you, an infinite soul,
experiencing their character as you are.

No one can be perfect,
as you will know when you read,
Your birth chart, your manual,
For THIS life that you lead.

Everyone has strengths and flaws,
As this is Earths law.
This is a training ground to experience IT ALL
in this life, and lives before.
We are here for a purpose, the same inner goal,
Some of us young in our soul journey,
And some of us old.

That's why you may have a young person,
wiser than their years.
That's why you may have an old person,
still inflicting violence and tears.

As a young soul there is much to learn…
So more mistakes are made, and many misbehave,
not considering their actions a concern.

How we can help is to protect others and send love,
'Plug in' to the surplus of energy below and above.
To connect with Mother Earth and Father Sky,
Is like connecting to the mains where vaults are high!

Let go, be present, allow the waves of love through you,
Absorb this energy, relax- enjoy your new world view.

You can learn to harness and direct this energy too…
Through the martial arts of Qi Gong and Kung Fu.

Qi Gong is the Yin,
The soft, the healing.
Kung Fu is the Yang,
The warrior, the protector from gangs.

To be balanced, do both,
Help your soul's growth!
Be able to heal yourself and others,
But also, take no sh*t.
Then the game you won't quit.
You will have more strength, connection…
learn to harness universal energy
and your life will be lit!

The wonders we can do with energy by good intention,
We can transform the world, just by love and attention.

We are powerful and we can make a difference,
Energy affects everything,
it can dissolve ignorance.

Now working with energy takes perseverance.
It takes being present, in our senses,
openness and of course,
persistence.

But once achieved,
Our minds will be at ease,
Suffering deceased,
Stress and sadness decreased.

It aids a positive response from our inner soul
to our characters hard times,
Understanding that what we face,
are our missions,
for this lifetime.

When our minds and inner selves are at peace,
That's when we co-create!
 A beautiful external world
-we impact the game!

We will stumble and make some mistakes,
As we're learning in the process!
So be kind to yourself,
eat some cakes (in moderation).

Relax, let go
and trust in it all.
Zoom out, remember,
it's a game after all…

A Game we chose to come here and play…
Rediscover your soul mission.
Ask for guidance.
Pray.

My Avatar

A little insight into my avatar: I am a Libra Sun, Sagittarius Moon and Scorpio Rising. Leo Mars, Aries Saturn, Libra Mercury.

With Pluto in Sagittarius in my first house, the stars indicate that I am "fuelled by intense energy and a love for exploration and expansion". (Relatable). This placement suggests that I have a "magnetic presence" and a profound desire to uncover truth and meaning in life. (Also a bit of a risk taker!). Pluto's influence in the first house signifies a journey marked by intensity and transformation—a journey where every challenge is a chance to evolve and become the best version of myself.

Intense experiences have shaped me in profound ways, pushing me beyond my limits and leading to profound personal growth and regeneration. Some I will share in this book as they have taught me resilience, strength, and the power of embracing change. When I reflected on my life and the series of challenges I have experienced, yet always bounce back from, this helped me understand the true purpose of this book... to express my own challenging experiences and share what helped me to find strength to rise from the ashes, with the intention that you may connect and relate to some or all of the experiences and take ideas to support your own healing and expansion. I am sure everyone can relate to intense experiences changing them in some way. We have all overcome great challenges. We have all felt broken and deep emotional pain. And we can all support each other to heal in the process.

I only had this understanding recently (March 2024), however I have added this insight in here to help set the scene.

I also recently learned about 'Human design', another interesting system which explains more about our character, again, based on date, location and time of birth. This system explains I am a 'Projector' with my only fixed energy centres being my third eye and my throat. In short summary, I speak my truth but with so many open centres I take on and reflect the environment I am in (physically and socially). I think this is why I often enjoy alone time to recentre myself. I recommend looking into this too if you are interested to learn more about your avatar in this current life.

When I was younger, I loved watching the series 'Avatar: The Last Airbender'. I could never decide which element I felt most connected to, as I resonate with them all: Air, Fire, Water, Earth. Each element reflects different parts of me, and they remind me of the diverse healing modalities found in cultures around the world. Just as each element plays a vital role in the balance of nature, I believe that exploring a variety of practices can help us heal and find balance within ourselves. The more I dive into exploring different practices, the more informed I become in my own hybrid approach to life, integrating what resonates with me from different viewpoints and healing modalities, from around the world.

As a kid, I was drawn to martial arts through Jackie Chan cartoons, which sparked my passion and led me to join Little Ninjas and Taekwondo.

At 11, I was further inspired by 'Kung Fu Panda', who became somewhat a role model for me—embodying the warrior and the healer, the balance of yin and yang, all while bringing humour into life, which I believe is so important. This ultimately fuelled my fascination with the martial arts of Kung Fu and Qi Gong, which then came into my life further down the line.

In terms of my hobbies, I like to engage in Qi Gong, Kung Fu, Spiritual practices and explore nature with my dog/ best friend, Kody. I like writing poems and they have been a healing and transformational journey of expression for me, helping me to understand (somewhat) the craziness and beauty of this life experience. I also love to have exciting new adventures and wacky experiences, finding things and activities off the beaten track. I love to explore the world!

I am a trained Occupational Therapist, a person-centred holistic profession in mainstream healthcare practice, looking at peoples emotional, physical, mental and spiritual health, their environment and the impact this has on them and the 'occupation' (meaningful activity) they want to engage with. Occupations give our life meaning and come into three categories- self-care, productivity, and leisure. To have good health and wellbeing we need to be balanced in all these areas. Occupational Therapists help people to engage in the occupations that are meaningful to them by overcoming barriers and increasing engagement and independence. It is an interesting and diverse profession and covers a variety of fields and settings such as community, mental health hospitals, physical health hospitals, prisons, schools and more. Occupational Therapy applies to every human being and I often 'OT myself'.

I began really writing poems when I went through the loss of a great friendship and guide, an intense and world-shattering grief, a pain like no other I had experienced. I was 23 at the time. It was this intense grief which led me to the woods to heal and express through writing; poetry was my release and my healing. My best friend and companion was present with me for most poems that I wrote- his name is Kody, and he is a Border collie dog. We would spend hours and hours daily in the woods. He has been in my life for 10 years and is the love of my life. Kody accompanied me throughout my grief, loving me unconditionally, despite my intense emotions, and prevented me from resorting to complete isolation. He is a great teacher to me, teaching me to be present and happy and focus on my senses. Keep things simple, no need for complexity. Dogs are so precious.

My words helped me to heal myself and the poems were written initially for me. I would sit with the trees, and just let the words flow through my pen. I could be sat in the same spot for hours writing until I finished the poem. Very few if any changes have been made to these poems as most are left the raw version. I like to read them whenever I am feeling in a dark hole (especially the ones with no obvious cause) and I find they boost my mood and lift me out of any heaviness feelings, helping me to let go and bring my focus back to the present moment, gratitude, and to hold a feeling of curiosity towards this experience we call 'life' and to remind myself of what I already know, but sometimes forget in times of darkness.

My Avatars shadow? Indecision, taking on too much and becoming overwhelmed, being 'spread too thin', poor memory, can be shy and hold back, can care too much what others think, can be poor at communicating (when in a state of overwhelm), can doubt myself, not seeing red flags, appearing naïve. Aware of it all, accepting and striving to be my best self, and guess what? I still love me. My shadow would not exist without my light.

I feel incredibly thankful for the life I've been blessed with.

I'm grateful for my good health, the love of my family, and the safe environment I've always had the privilege of growing up in.

There are of course challenges, however my basic needs have always been taken care of, either by my family or through my own efforts. I've never had to go without food for extended periods, and I've been fortunate to have a roof over my head most of the time. I have not lived in war.

I recognise how fortunate I am, and my heart goes out to those who are less fortunate in these aspects. I send my love, respect, and positive energy, hoping for brighter days ahead for everyone.

As a global community, despite our different cultures, environments, beliefs, and experiences, there is more that connects us than divides us. Our shared humanity is reflected in the emotions we all experience. I'm sure there are times when everyone has felt sadness, anger, anxiety, fear, guilt, shame, love, joy, connection, trust, support, ecstasy, excitement, fulfilment, and pride—the deepest of dark emotions to the lightest of light. It is through these emotions that we can relate to each other, regardless of the perceived surface-level differences.

The first couple of poems of this book are to set the scene; they were not my first written poems, but I feel they are a good introduction to this book, and some of my personal favourites!

2. 'The Beautiful You' 22.03.2021

Hey you there… I SEE you.
Now for a journey of discovery,
Treasures of life your heart will see,
But first let's address the tragedy.

Look at the world around you, it's dumbfound to,
Think we're gunna pull it all down to
'fulfill our needs'?
…or fulfil our greeds.

Pain and anger.
Everywhere you look left…
Everywhere you look right…
But the future can be bright-
If for peace we fight!

Trust me you have power…
In this golden age hour…
Don't be a T.V. cauliflower!

You are not alone, ancestors guide you,
Your number one supporters,

The ultimate life sorters,
Calming life's troubled waters.

They know all you do
and they always love you,
no judgement, no fear,
just let them near,
ask out loud,
say it clear and proud,
so they can help your dreams come true.

Don't feel shy or silly,
open your mind- see the value
they will guide you when you don't have a clue!
Trust, the feeling in your gut,
let messages come through...
this is spirit guiding you.

Marvel at the world.
Can you smell the flowers?
Stare at the sky for hours?
Use your senses- be empowered!
and I don't mean,
the senses in your head.

See life must be in balance,
Strength and love enhanced,

No longer silenced…
All peace no violence.

Connect with the Earth,
bare foot on the grass,
Send energetic roots deep down,
Yes it's true there are waves of energy,
That we can feel but we cannot see.

Just like the waves between radio and telly,
Do you think humans are less capable than machines?
Experience for yourself is the only way to see,
Waves of sensation flowing through your body.

Then…
love and joy!
Everywhere you look left,
Everywhere you look right,
Everyone is alright,
Ready to take flight.

So put the mind to bed
and by spirit you'll be led
to the peace and joy
inside
the beautiful you.

That was the first poem I wrote to an instrumental beat I listened to on repeat (inspired by a man I worked with at the mental health hospital, whose passion was rap, and we worked towards him getting to the recording studio in the town- he did so good!). I had so much to say but I had to be concise. I invite you to use your imagination to explore the thought trains I was on.

Self-Care Toolkit

Throughout my life I have tried a variety of things to support my health and wellbeing. The next poem is a short summary of some of these techniques. When I was writing it, I realised I have created my own 'Self-care toolkit' which I go to during times of need and also just for daily maintenance (after learning that prevention is better than cure). I have a daily routine I do in the morning when I wake up and it was making this a daily habit, which has helped me greatly and always sets me up well for the day ahead.

That said, I have also learned to be kind to myself on the days where I do not complete my morning practices, which happens when my routine is off. Learning to be gentle with ourselves is key and a crucial component of the 'self-care toolkit'. Ensuring a quick 'I Love You' eye to eye in the mirror, setting the intention for a positive day and feeling grateful are game changers during those days where I only have 5 minutes.

I encourage you to think about what things you have or would like to have in your self-care toolkit, and create a selection of techniques, activities and practices unique to you (which can be done any time of day). This toolkit can be in your mind, or you could draw, write or craft a physical self-care toolkit. I have found it to be super empowering and a reminder of how much influence we can have on our health, our day, our perspective and our opportunities. They say it takes 21 days of doing something consistently for it to become a natural part of our daily life.

3. 'Self-Care Toolkit' 22.03.2022

Ok… let's talk medicine.
Have an open mind, let knowledge in.
This system is not all caring,
Pharmaceutical packets they've got us tearing!

Ancient teachings, need sharing…
You are your healing,
it's your power they've been stealing.
But trust,
you are the real thing!
Vibrations heal,
so use your voice- sing!

Sound frequencies are cleansing,
With music, souls be blending.
Healthy lifestyle, fitness, diet
Your Earth body needs tending!

Observe your mind do your thoughts need mending?
Thoughts manifest, so what have you got pending?
To the negative thoughts, put an ending,

Release the pain, let your light bulb ding
...
Or even dong,
You can't go wrong,
when you follow your heart song.
You have power like King Kong,
Flip the switch of expansion on.

Now let's talk meditation.
Focus your attention,
hold your intention...
Expand from this dimension!
Just release the tension,
Come into your senses
Breathe...
and suprasense it!
No more suspension,
Did I mention?
...
Now's the time of the ascension!
Now's the time of the ascension...

Many methods you can use,
Here, I will list a few:
Qi gong, yoga, kindness, creativity
Cold showers, gratitude,
Plant teacher ceremony

The ancient medicines, can show the way,
Guiders, supporters, listen to what they say,
But remember you yourself are the ultimate medicine!
Don't rely on external input for your ascension.

You must put in the work...
Daily holistic practices.
Morning routine
Is a space
to begin these things.

Imagine you have just woken up

Open your eyes, deep breath in
...
And smile to the ceiling!
You are alive today
What a miraculous thing!
Many did not wake up today...
But you did!

Start this moment with a heart full of gratitude.
Gratitude leads to expansion, large magnitude!
Get out of bed, drink some water
Hydrate your body like you know you ought ta!

Reach, bend, stretch,

Awaken your physical.

Release blockages,

balance back to equal.

Sit on the floor, be still in meditation,

Even just one minute will raise your vibration!

Set your days intention,

send love out and PRAY.

You are your creator.

The world's oyster awaits ya

… Each day!

Remove internal barriers…

Then of magic we are carriers!

Self-belief and trust is essential…

We are so influential!

Build your physical strength, do some exercise,

Strength and flex helps a lot in this life,

It makes daily living much easier,

As the body is more equipped to deal with it

…

Throw Qi Gong in the mix!
Guide the flow of energy,
Under the cloak of invisibility,
To your organs, emotions, spirit...
bring tranquillity!
This is a tool in your took kit, see?

I'm talking tool kit of self-care,
We use this to cleanse, heal, prepare....

You can use the above suggestions,
Or your own with pure intentions.
You are the keeper of your soul's home.
Right decisions your gut knows.
Just release and go,
with the flow.
Go with the flow,
Go with the flow,
Flow.

Ideas to put in your Self-Care Toolkit

I will share some ideas of things I have tried and use as part of my self-care toolkit.

Things for me are: Meditation, Qi Gong, Kung Fu, walking in nature, time with my dog, Kody, writing a gratitude diary, working out, yoga, writing poems, journaling, healthy food, breathwork, cold showers, wild swimming, reading, adventures and spending time and connecting with family, friends and loved ones.

Also, marmalade on sourdough toast, lie ins, baths, chocolate, fun adventures, new experiences, and movie nights too! All about balance and moderation, and this is a constant journey, and it is easy for us to slip, so when this happens, the best we can do is to be gentle and kind to ourselves. We do not need to be 100% all the time, as this is impossible. Be gentle and celebrate small wins of things that can easily slip into daily routine and may be as quick as a one-minute meditation to do some deep breaths or looking in the mirror and saying 'I love you, I got you, today is a great day, thank you'.

An app called 'Insight timer' has many meditations, poems and uplifting talks, has been a great tool for me. In terms of reading, books which have had extreme positive influence over my life include: The 'Celestine prophecy' (and all its sequels), 'The Secret', 'Brida', 'Rise and Shine', 'You can Heal your Body' and 'The Alchemist'.

It is also important to be balanced in what we engage in, and it definitely makes me feel good to be balanced in my self-care, leisure and productivity. Occupational therapy showed me the importance of this.

Other helpers for me include vitamins, minerals and Bach flowers. Boosting vitamin C (immune system and much more) with Camu Camu powder (a great high source of Vit C), vitamin D, sea moss, alkaline based diet, cayenne pepper and Celtic Sea salt and others I find helpful for me (although I must admit I am not consistent in taking them every day!).

In 2023 I had a serious case of inflammation in my body. This was a very traumatic and challenging time, lots of pain and uncertainty. One evening I was at my friend's recording studio in London, and he called me an uber back to where I was staying as I was suddenly very hot and in extreme pain. In the Uber I was panicking, and the driver began chatting with me. I ended up sharing I was feeling anxious and not good in my body and did not know if this was serious and needed action, having been into A and E a couple of times already. He very calmly explained to me that I have inflammation and can help reduce it by making a green juice every morning. The green juice included green apples, two raw cabbage leaves and ginger blended with water and sieved. He then took me to a shop to buy the ingredients. He was so kind and this had a huge influence on my healing journey over the summer. I feel the green juice was crucial for my healing.

My ideal drinks morning routine includes the following:

In the morning:

Have a pint of warm water- to hydrate, kick start digestive fire (that's why it's warm) and flush system

Alkaline: Have a pint of warm water with added:

Lime squeezed

Celtic sea salt (pinch)

Cayenne pepper (pinch)

Alkaline: Blend and filter/ juice:

2 x green granny smith apples

1 x large leafy cabbage leaf

Big chunk of ginger

Juice of lemon or lime

Water

Optional extras for green juice:

Coriander/ parsley (helps to detox heavy metals out of the body)

Dandelion leaves (helps cleanse the kidneys- make sure to drink plenty of water throughout the day to flush them through)

Seamoss (contains most of the minerals our body needs)

Camu camu powder (great form of vitamin C)

Bach flowers were developed by Dr Bach in the 1920's. They are 38 natural remedies to address the emotional and mental imbalances humans can experience. The essences are derived from nature- plants and trees and each address a specific imbalance. For example, it is said that 'Pine' helps decrease Guilt, 'Larch' to build confidence, 'Star of Bethlehem' helps recover from trauma, 'Wild Oat' helps for uncertainty of correct path in life. The most well-known one is 'rescue remedy' which is a combination of 5 of the Bach flowers and is used to help reduce anxiety. It includes Cherry plum (mental breakdown), Rock water (terror), Star of Bethlehem (grief or trauma), Impatiens (impatience) and Clematis (dreamy state). Bach flowers are super powerful when taken consistently and the right dose. They have helped me a lot.

Pharmaceuticals do have their place. They do the job in allowing us to continue to function, especially when we are in times of serious imbalance or crisis. Much respect and gratitude to those who work with these tools to save lives and increase quality of life for people. I have taken pharmaceuticals, and I will take them again when I need to, especially during health crisis.

All I am saying is that sometimes there are other solutions and avenues to try, and people should be given all of the information and the options before they must choose a treatment to engage in, particularly for minor imbalances. I express my observation that when pharmaceuticals are used as a long-term solution to an imbalance, the root cause is not addressed, just the symptoms suppressed. So when the medication is stopped, the symptoms return, and often worse, leading to more medication... for life.

Holistic methods, although are the long game, are great to address the root cause and are extremely powerful in the prevention of imbalance and supporting of re-balance. The Earth provides all medicines we need, from herbs, to plants, to fruits and foods, to ancient practices dating back through the history of the Earth.

To explore these whilst feeling good as well as when you are not feeling good is recommended. Always go with what feels right for you, just make sure you know what options are available to you for different health challenges that arise and always seek advice if you are not sure which way to turn. Some things can counteract each other so it is important to check. For example, grapefruit can lower blood pressure, but it is dangerous to eat this when taking pharmaceutical medication to lower blood pressure. If you are taking medication, always check with a health professional what can be explored safely.

For a clear list of these practices, please refer to the Self-Care toolkit appendix, on pg. 326.

***

The next poem is the oldest one I found and is to My Grandad, a great friend and rock in my life, who passed away in 2018.

4. 'Poem for Grandad' 12.02.2019

Grandad, it's been a year since you past,

And a crazy time it has been too,

You wouldn't believe some of the mad things I have learned, experienced and discovered,

And still I know many things are to be discovered.

I miss your laugh, I miss your smile,

I miss your hugs, I miss your open ears,

I miss your humour, I miss our cuddles,

Gosh it feels like it's been years.

You always were my strong steady rock,

Un-swayed by all my fears,

You taught me strength, courage, wisdom,

You brought me up from tears.

I think about you often,

I feel you near me too,

When I meditate and touch my heart,

I feel light and know it's you.

I know you're watching me,

 and all that I go through,

I can see you cheering me on saying

'Come on Lu!'

Gone but never forgotten,

you are a crucial part of me,

I see you in the sunsets

and in the old oak tree.

I love you so much,

that's the main thing I have to say,

So cheers to you in heaven,

I hope to meet you there some day.

5. Poem for Grandad: '2 years since...'
12.02.2020

It's been 2 years since you left us,

I have much more to tell you because,

I've had a new job, new experiences, new adventures,

I've learned more healing and more cures.

I love and miss you daily- that will never change

In the future a big catch up we must arrange.

My confidence and strength have grown and grown,

I now can feel at peace when I am alone.

For now I send you positivity, strength and love.

I know you are watching over me

from beyond the skies above.

The Healer

I wish to share a bit about Jim, whose death inspired and led me to really explore and delve into expressing myself through poetry back in 2020.

Jim was a rare soul. A Camden man from London, born healer and psychic and enhanced his skills learning from a range of people and self-taught methods. He achieved life's aim of achieving that perfect balance between hard and soft. He was a master in martial arts and was fearless and protective, an old school gangster, accounting for the 'hard'. Jim was dedicated to his martial arts of Kung Fu and Qi Gong, street fighting and was a master swordsman in Samurai.

Yet he was also a holistic healer, seeing people for the light that lies within, teaching ways of love and peace and harmony- the 'soft'. People used to say that he could save you or he could kill you. Not a man you want to cross but such an asset to have on your side and in your life. Jim was a medicine man, understanding the healing properties of a vast variety of herbs, flowers, plants and foods. He could shake your hand and know everything about you. He could see 'the invisible world' (spirits), read minds and had visions of the future.

Jim travelled to the Peru Jungle where he shared his knowledge with the powerful shamans there. He was presented with a pipe referred to as a pipe carrier, a very high honour. Through smoke ceremonies he could communicate with the Great Spirit and light beings to get answers and messages. He did not need to take master medicines to get to the spiritual planes, he could get there without.

He was also known as a powerful healer and medicine man in North Dakota by the Native Americans, engaging in powerful and transformational sweat lodges there.

There was nothing he found too challenging, and he always had an idea and let his intuition guide him. I witnessed him on numerous occasions extract toxins or excess fat from organs through a shamanic practice which he did un-invasively, using water in his mouth, which blew my mind!

Jim and I became close when I was 19, as what I witnessed through his healing on my friend, who was in health crisis, fascinated me greatly. It was then that I realised there IS magic in this world. We became great friends and he then completed healings on me and my family too. He told me I too have natural healing hands and that I could develop this skill through practicing the martial art of Qi Gong which I then began to learn with him.

Jim had developed his own style of Qi Gong, calling it 'freestyle Qi Gong'. This included some things he had learned from his masters, adapting them in some cases, in addition to developing his own movements and sequences, which he could see, and feel were beneficial for health and wellbeing due to his psychic abilities. It is different to any other Qi Gong I have come across. This was not recorded anywhere as he had an incredible memory and had it all in his head.

Jim changed my life and got me onto the right path and for that I am so incredibly grateful. The knowledge he shared with me enabled me to bring my health and wellbeing into my own hands and learn and apply the healing powers of Qi Gong as a sustainable healthcare intervention. I told him the importance of sharing his style of Qi Gong more widespread as it could benefit so many people and he agreed that if I could do the writing part (he was more street wise than academic), we could start to do this. He is the source, so this wisdom is fresh and relevant to society and our bodies in present day. Our connection was deep and was the most powerful and magnificent thing I have ever experienced.

During his astral travels, Jim had visions and insights and spoke of a looming darkness—the precursor to a global pandemic. He told me all about Covid-19 before it began. He engaged in astral travel every night, as he is part of the high spirit counsel, to devise strategies aimed at preventing potential harmful events.

As fate would have it, his calling in the spiritual world grew stronger, and on Easter Sunday 2020, he left us…

leaving a void that echoed with the loss of a dear friend, mentor, and guide.

In the midst of grief, guided by an unspoken promise, I undertook the responsibility of preserving his legacy. Jim's teachings on Qi Gong and healing techniques are valuable tools for self-preservation, representing a significant part of his lasting gift to the world.

This narrative, though fantastical to some, is my truth and is a tribute to a man who, in life and beyond, shaped destinies, healed souls, and left a lasting impact on those fortunate enough to cross his path. I know I will be unlikely to meet another soul like him in this life time.

As I embark on the journey of sharing his wisdom through the Qi Gong and healing techniques he showed me, I invite you to join me in honouring the life of Jim—a guardian of ancient knowledge, a healer of profound abilities, and a cherished soul who illuminated the path to higher realms.

In heartfelt gratitude, I extend a thank you—from my soul to yours.

AHO.

***

***

The poems ahead are presented in the chronological order of their creation, inviting you to accompany me on my poetic journey. Together, we will witness the ebbs and flows—the highs and lows—mirroring the rhythm of life that we all experience in our unique way.

Some poems may shine brighter, while others offer a more subtle glow, but each contributes to my evolving journey. Join me in embracing challenges and opportunities and exploring and expressing my life experience. I am just another little human, exploring and walking my path in this world, making mistakes, making successes, and learning a little more about what it means to be alive, each day.

The following poem was written 10 days after Jim's passing, and is the beginning of this journey.

6. 'Passing Poem' 22.04.2020

I can't believe this day has come…
The day you left the Earth and flew,
Sky high up into heaven and the light above…
But oh, we had so much more to do.

I know this darkness will become less,
And I hear you voice in my ear saying 'don't stress'.
But right now the pain is real and deep.
However, I am so grateful for the memories I keep.

For in this life we found each other and shared a deep love.
The type of connection and love only experienced up above.
We brought it down to this level on Earth and for a short while
had perfect harmony,
It was short and sweet but ours forever to keep, even now
you're free.

You are so special and that's why you were taken,
Taken to the spiritual realm to lessen the hating.
You are so magical and skilled and kick ass,
And have a heart of gold that will always last.

You were the ripple which started the wave of many,
Opening eyes, hearts and minds a plenty.

Oh positive Jim, seeing the bright side, lifting people up,
Pouring love, strength and knowledge into empty cups.
The world has changed by your presence here on it,
You spread love, light and wonder to all corners of it.

I already miss you more than words can say,
I just can't believe it, doubt I will any day.
I miss your voice, your eyes, your smile,
I miss your laughter, your jokes, your stories on file.
I miss your teachings, your guidance, your words of wisdom,
I miss your soul, your whole being… I miss all you've done.

Your love brought me out of the darkness and into the light.
Your knowledge taught me how to heal and how to fight.
I am still at the beginning of what you intended to teach me,
This makes me so sad as I just want to make you proud.
I hope we learn to communicate, please speak loud.

I'm so grateful for the love you gave me,
Not even joking, you saved me,
From the dark path I was heading down,
That was causing my spirit guide to frown.

You were understanding, always loving, never judging.
You were and are my rock- that will never stop.

The lessons you taught me will keep me grounded in years to come,
Don't worry I will stay on the path; your good work will not be undone.

We had so many adventures awaiting round the corner,
We'd planned Peru Jungle, North Dakota
and sharing healing retreats all over.
I want to still complete our adventures as a tribute to us,
I will be without you in person but will have you in spirit close.

I know this ain't my usual flow,
But I'm going through trauma as you know.

Luckily for me you built me up to be strong,
But right now I need to grieve,
it's too hard to bite my tongue.

I still feel you're around me, I feel your blessings and love,
Especially when I cleanse with the smoke,
I feel a beam in my head from above.
The feeling goes through my body
and brings me to my knees,
All I can do is sit and feel, staring at the trees.

I will keep learning and reach my destiny,
Just give me time to build my strength,
have faith in me.

I send you love and light for your new journey,
They are blessed to have you up there.
I know you will smash any task you're given,
And I know you'll always be fair.

I see you in the rivers, the bluebells and the old trees.
I feel you in the sunsets and smoke ceremonies.

One day I will see you again,
up there in the sky,
But I know I must be patient and fulfil my destiny,
Before it's my time to fly.

From my heart to your heart- AHO.

7. 'The Sun that Shines' 04.05.2020

The sun that shines.
The wind that blows.
The trees that whisper.
This is our home.

The rivers that wave.
The birds that fly.
The flowers that bloom.
A beautiful world, no lie.

The bee's that buzz.
The ants that scurry.
The fish that swim.
The humans that hurry.

We whiz and we dart
All of our lives its true.
Living life in the fast lane,
Not noticing morning dew.

But we are not grasping life's true essence,
To slow down and live in the present.

To notice the world around us,
Connect to it and let it ground us.

For the aim in life is to achieve the perfect balance,
Between mental, physical, spiritual and emotional strength.
Now this takes all our time and is the biggest challenge,
Whilst enjoying the high times and working through any trench.

The good times come and go,
As I'm sure you all know.
But the bad times will pass too.
Trust in the universe and you will get through.

Sit in a meadow,
Feel the breeze on your face.
Paddle in the sea,
Connect to others- embrace.

As love is what makes the world go round.
It is magical and spiritual, worth more than any pound.
It's love verses fear, now that is the true test,
But its up to you to choose, for this is your quest.

So for me I choose love,
Feeling it all around me, below and above.
It's beautiful like the loving bond of 2 doves,
And I will hold it inside, even when push comes to shove.

I am so grateful,
My future is bright.
I will do my bit to help heal this world,
For this I'm prepared to peacefully fight.

I know you are around me,
And within me too,
I will continue your legacy,
As a twin flame means 2.

8. 'One Month On' 12.05.2020

Sat in the bluebells,

Thinking of you.

This month has been crazy,

Sometimes feeling high, sometimes feeling blue.

Nature has helped me so much,

The greatest healer it's true.

I feel more connected to the Earth,

Which is helping me get through.

Right now the road ahead appears unknown,

I don't know what to do, or where to go...

But I have trust in the universe that I will be shown.

I will listen to the smoke and the intuitions as I blow.

The world vision seems blurry, a true mess.

But I must stay positive and not digress.

As that would mean letting the dark side win...

So instead I will take life's challenges on the chin and grin.

The world is full of love and beauty, when we train to see it,

And learning to use and feel energy is the best bit!

As once this is mastered,
it is a powerful toolkit,
To raise the vibration of the Earth,
and be rid of all the sh*t.

Trust me as I trust you,
I will do my best,
To live in love and light,
opening the magic chest.

I will do this always,
until I take my last breath,
until my spirit flies,
when it is my time to rest.

A year to process and progress

I continued working in the mental health hospital as an Occupational therapist for 6 months after Jim's passing and during the Covid-19 Pandemic. Every day I would walk and do Qi Gong in nature after work to clear my head and strengthen myself. The bluebells were so present in the Spring and I find them so magical and they held me greatly during my grieving process.

That summer I was invited to attend a 'Goddess Retreat' in Glastonbury, to offer energy healing and provide Qi gong classes in exchange for attending. I completed 7 healings in a row- using a mixture of shamanic healing, Qi Gong hands on healing and Reiki. I felt energy flow so much and a couple of the girls said they felt a powerful and protective man's presence. When I showed one of them a picture of Jim, she burst into tears and confirmed it was for sure him who she felt. This was an amazing experience for me as I felt so much energy flowing and I felt Jim helping and supporting me and to have this confirmed by someone else was so heart lifting. This experience was great, as before this I had only done healing on family and friends. I was amazed at the whole experience, what I felt and how the ladies felt who I did the healing on. It felt good to continue Jims's work and utilise what he taught me.

That summer I also went to my first spiritual festival with a conscious community... the Medicine festival. One of the only festivals to run during Covid. It was government approved as an experiment for how gatherings could work with Covid present- with only a few hundred people, no alcohol, wearing masks, social distancing and local council members to ensure the rules were followed! I heard about this through someone who attended the goddess retreat. Life's intricate chain of events at its finest.

I attended by myself, my first solo trip, and was blown away that there is such a spiritual community that exists! An alcohol-free event and a place you leave feeling much healthier than when you arrived. Very different to my previous festival experiences as a teenager of Leeds festival and Download festival which can be very heavy on drugs and alcohol and you feel close to death when you leave, needing a lot of recovery time! A whole new world opened up to me- of spiritual community. I had always just been very personal with my spirituality and explored this mainly by myself and with Jim. I was not aware there were so many people also on this path! I also felt so empowered that I went by myself and made many amazing connections!

I left the mental health hospital in November as I had a strong sense of urgency to write down and record as much of Jim's teachings of Qi Gong and healing that I could remember, as this was not recorded anywhere else. It was a hard decision to leave my job because I loved my team and the residents.

I moved back to my family home to complete this task I set myself to. I spent the following 6 months working a personal and 'full-time job', writing approximately 50,000 words of Jims teachings, going to the woods to record Qi Gong videos and this is the time when a lot of poetry had space to spring up. I felt Jims's support in spirit, helping me to remember as much Qi Gong as I did. There were the months of February and March especially when I could not help but write poems in the woods for hours with Kody, as I was feeling my most creative self.

Writing a poem for my Grandad began this intense period of poetry.

9. 'Grandad, 3 years on' 12.02.2021

Dear Grandad, I hope all is well with you,

That you're working and chilling with the angels,

lots of laughter too.

I think about you often and cherish our memories,

Some of these moments shared with friends,

And some with family.

You continue to guide us in present times,

Lessons and wisdom shared in the past,

helping us to shine.

 You help in other ways now too,

The uplifting signs of spirit,

A white feather, or a robin,

lifts me out of the blue.

I feel you close in the conservatory,

the Zen Garden you built,

and all around the farm,

And feel your humour, care and sweet charm.

Grief is a hard thing,

it never truly goes,

But understanding you're still around,

my spirit knows.

I know but this life is but a flash,

in the grand scheme of things...

What a miracle to experience this life on a beautiful planet

fit for kings!

I have peace knowing the true you is not gone,

My heart is lightened knowing I will see you again before long.

Please continue to guide us,

your family and friends here on Earth,

Protect us, uplift us, give us strength,

Help us discover our true worth.

Cheers to you, 3 years in the Great Light

10.'At One with the Pine Tree' 14.02.2021

Water drops roll down my cheeks,
releasing the grief.
Water drops now fall from the heavens above…
I feel magic and love as they embrace my face
and become one with me.

I sit on a rock,
Level with the pine trees at their mid-top.
I hear them whispering and creaking in the wind,
I see them dancing and swaying,
they are having an Earth sing.

Wavy at the top,
Yet perfectly still at the bottom-
The connectors between Earth and Heaven.

Such a large community- the tree,
I feel humbled in their presence,
They are huge giants compared to me!

Oh to experience life at such a zoomed in perspective,
How wonderful, unique- we are the collective.

As tree is me,
And I is tree,
We are in the same extended family.
That family that everything and all belong to,
The family of the Great Spirit, it's true.

When we train to let go, it makes life easy,
not queasy.
It is so simple yet is our biggest challenge,
We must use our mental strength,
instead of being singed.

Singed by the fires of hatred and envy,
The fires of violence, inequality, fear, frenzy.
These things take their toll on our ability to let go,
To truly surrender to the universe and merge with the flow.
For this you need to develop true trust.
Have faith, self believe, and love is a must!

May instead the fires of light, love and peace
blaze in your presence,
Shining and spreading light to all the four nations,
To every inch of Mother Earth, Father Sky
and all of Creation.

This is why we came to this Earth,

To develop love, trust and belief in the light.

To connect within to allow the ultimate connection,

Blocking its way is our self- the true fight.

Our ego, our mind, our lack of self-love,

Our inability to rest and experience the only time that truly matters in our life's...

The present moment.

11. 'Choosing to be a Warrior, not a Victim'
15.02.2021

The stillness of self,
The tweeting bird sounds,
The stillness of clouds,
 Hey peace you can be found!

The silenced mind,
The relaxed limbs and muscles,
Awareness at its peak,
No hustle or bustle.

To find peace is an achievement,
To find it when in joy, anger, fear and bereavement.
To find it when feeling glamorous, sad, flamboyant,
To find it, be it, become it- not fraudulent.

When this new baseline is mastered,
its life mission accomplished!
Then spread it and share it to the world and those in anguish.

Balanced Flame

Where light shines,
No darkness can prevail,
It's like comparing Usain bolt to a Snail!

Oh peace within, oh peace without,
I sure love your company, without a doubt!

The fire in me is always burning.
I choose to feed it positivity, gratitude and love,
As when I feed it other things,
it gets pretty concerning!

To feed the fire with fear and sad,
To feed into the belief that I am mad,
Does nothing but reduce my fire to a smoulder,
Although the fires never out,
It carries the weight of a boulder!

Now walking around with a boulder inside,
Feels like I'm swimming against a strong ass tide!

Every day a struggle, no one to cuddle,
I feel like sh*t... pass me a shovel.

I may as well bury myself, dig my own grave.
I am sick of the system and being a slave.

But then a realisation occurs… my slave driver, biggest enemy?
It's the negative me!
Now I can't blame society, nor political parties,
I can only blame myself and my internal stories.

Stories of believing I am a worthless victim…
To become aware is to forgive self and put these stories in the bin.

And realise myself that I am the creator,
Of my life- Yes, I can shape it!

As my awareness grows and I become my true self,
I wipe the negativity away from my brain shelf.

I proceed to shelve my positivity, joy and love,
As I do this I connect to the light beam from above.

Down this beam comes waves of love and connectivity,
To and from the Great Spirit, the angels,
And loved ones I can't see.

I become lighter and lighter,
The fire inside brighter and brighter,
I become a solid yet peaceful fighter,
The blanket of love gets tighter.

It lifts me out of the grave I once self-dug,
It lifts me off down the street, past the community hub,
It lifts me higher as we head above.

I float up and up out into space,
Beautiful colours and stars, a breath-taking picture.
I look back on Earth and the human race,
I think to myself 'how can we fix this place?'

Angels and guides appear at my side, all with sticks like wands,
They pass me one.
They say to envision a planet in love and balance,
In equality, freedom and sustainable bamboo pants!

I do as they say and start straight away,
Using the fire inside to guide me.
A zap of humour, good health, a connected Earth family.

Qi Gong and healing as mainstream knowledge,
No need to spend years learning it at college,
As it is taught a young age in the tribal family,
The one you belong to, and you…and you… and me.

Mother Earth is thriving, in balance, so happy.
Father Sky is balanced, natural disasters I can't see!

All is well and well is all,
Life now an understood miracle.

I hand back my wand, give thanks and float back to Earth...
I know now how much life is worth.

My fire I must keep blazing inside me,
To envision the world in balance and act- using my vision to guide me.

The choice I have made now to be a warrior, not a victim,
I believe in myself.
Thank God that's clicked in!

12. 'Spirit Message' 17.02.2021

This poem is very long, a non-stop stream of writing that I wrote one afternoon in the woods. I have split it into parts to make it more digestible.

'Spirit message' Part 1

It's not me who's talking,

Its spirit coming through

To give you some guidance on what you can do.

Relax. Take a breath.

Detach from emotions and stress.

Use your senses and experience the world around you.

The colours, the textures,

The occasional moo.

Can you feel the wind on your face?

The warmth of the sun on your body?

Can you feel energy from the tree you embrace?

Can you feel your limbs, your organs, aware of your body?

The body is your home in a home.

One home is the Earth, shared with all,

And the other you have to yourself alone.

This personal home is your body,

A temple just for you

You're in charge of the upkeep

And what you feed it too.

Choose to feed it with processed foods, sugar and too much beer,

And it becomes a hotel you wouldn't want to go near!

Feed it with anger, hatred and stress,

It won't function properly

And it won't rest.

What you experience in this body alone,

Is reflected to you out in the Earth home,

If all beings were to do this,

Earth becomes a no-go zone!

As what will be created in the world is imbalance,

hunger, un-happiness,

With some resorting to violence,

more sadness

Those who do are living in fear.
It's not their fault,
their life is unclear.

We engage in toxins
As escapism from the matrix we live in.
Examples are alcohol, fake foods, processed sugar,
These poison our body, so belong in the bin!

For our body home, the responsibility lies with only us,
To do the cleaning, the upkeep and our minds we must relax.

However, the Earth home is home to all,
Which is its greatest feature,
But also its greatest downfall.

As a home which has many occupants,
Can become messy, chaotic and full of disagreements.

This can be a recipe for an unhappy home.
Occupants disconnected, greedy and trying to live alone.
The home is abused, Mother Earth groans.
But there is another way…we can be shown.

Our personal home, our bodies, we must first put right,
As only then do we stand a chance to shine out as a light.
A peaceful fight, but strength is essential,

To face our shadows and let go,
This will bring out our potential!
Now this refurbishment ain't easy,
But when heading in the right direction,
Life becomes more breezy.

Coincidences left, right and forwards,
The present moment always with us and before us.

Sitting back and experiencing life from the perspective of our small body home,
Finding joy and learning from the lessons we are shown.

Learning from challenges and pain,
Boosts our soul level up,
Like a video game,
Where your character wins a gold cup.

7 times we must come down and 7 times we must go up,
As there are 7 levels of heaven, to work our way up.

Once at the top, complete freedom and bliss,
You don't have to come back to Earth,
You can give that one a miss!

That's because Earth is on a low-ish vibration,
The midpoint between hell and heaven.

The training ground for souls if you like,
Angel's one team of helpers,
Demons the other team, who like frights and fights.
Both teams have the same goal,
To claim souls to take above or below.

***

Beware of the temptations of current society,
Currently the dark side have more control,
blocking us from being free.

Temptations of alcohol and poisoned foods,
Temptations to judge others and be stuck in bad moods.
Temptations of money, diamonds and riches.
Temptations of 'getting all the b*tches'.
Temptations of overworking to feel like you matter.
Temptations of wasting food on a silver platter.

These temptations come with the slogan 'happiness and joy',
But they are short lived and slowly our spirit they destroy.

Our lifestyle causing Mother Nature's disharmony
Like our single use plastic ending up in the sea.

A weak spirit combined with the blind fold we have over our eyes,

Causes us to act without compassion, handing ourselves to the dark side.

To work with the realm of the angels takes more strength than this,

It takes courage, commitment and aware-ness.

…

But this provides many gifts.

Look out for small signs, coincidences, a feather.

Look out for repeating numbers or interesting sensations,

Do this forever.

Make time to be quiet and sit,

We come through in the silent and present moment bits.

As society has trained us to look to the future or the past,

Which causes anxiety and depression, heavy in our hearts.

This makes the job of the angels even harder,

But when human souls are present, angels can speak louder.

They may speak not with words,

Instead with energy and sensations not heard.

They may be seen by some,

Or felt as a feeling in the heart,

as many have done-

You don't have to be 'smart'.

Just be present, connect and feel,
Get in the flow of life's wheel,
Be as strong as steel,
Yet as soft as an eel.

The balance of hard and soft,
Be the warrior, the healer,
Give and receive love a lot.

Don't force things, trust the process, allow things to be,
Like Buddha, Gandhi and Mohammed Ali.

From this place your projections onto the Earth home are much better,
Your mind impacts everything, even the weather.

As you are now a light being,
On our dear planet,
Working your way to Heaven,
Spreading peace while you're at it!

Making this level of the game easier on Earth,
Helping current beings and future souls who here will birth.

'Spirit message' Part 2

As mentioned above, there are 7 levels in this game,
But to get to the next one,
Knowledge must be gained.

Knowledge almost lost in our current way of living,
Too many unaware,
too many give in.

For each level you must work up each chakra,
And at any time the temptations of the dark side could have ya!.
Each level may take one lifetime,
But most likely take many.
Our minds wiped each time,
So we don't carry over revenge or envy.
Our hearts are born pure so the worlds magic we can see.

Imagination of children is their strength,
which is blessed.
They can see things we can't as adults,
as our minds have been messed.

We must empower the children to share their knowledge,
The most recent beings from heaven…
So wisdom of spirit still fresh in their minds, like they've
graduated from heaven college.

The connectors of the bridge,

The bridge between heaven and Earth for where souls travel,

Souls full of excitement and adventure ready for their next life challenge.

As before they come they pick their journey,

A journey to provide the necessary learning,

The learning needed to try and level soul up,

The challenges they must face and never give up.

***

Now I never said this game was easy,

else it would not be this game.

A game so hard to comprehend with our little brain.

Few become a master,

For others it can be a disaster!

But for most of us we keep on learning,

Each day and night, our fire inside burning.

I know it's hard to comprehend,

That when your body dies it's not the end!

No my dear, the 'end' is to transcend,

To expand, whizz, bend!

Even the first level of heaven is complete bliss,
And rumour has it you can stay there if you wish.

When you die you become your higher self,
The self who knows all past lives,
Past husbands, children and wives.
The self who knows you inside and out,
Your whole soul journey, not just the chapter you're in now.

Wow higher self, take a bow,
You really got me like wow!
The awe raising my brows.
This blows my mind more than Mentos in coke,
Yet as the dust settles, I see through the smoke.

My higher self is me; I am part of her.
I can connect with her anytime,
Through patience, sensations and words.
The more I maintain the light in me,
She becomes easier to feel, hear and see.

The more time I make,
to make space,
For this grace,
I am better placed
In the race
of existence.

Show up for yourself,
make mistakes, don't be late,
But you can't be late as the time is the now,
It's a place where you always are,
So you can relax that frown!

We all get distracted,
Just don't stray too far.
Enjoy the life you're living,
Have fun, dance and sing,

Just remember who you truly are- that awareness within.
If all this is new to you- let the magic begin!

'Spirit message' Part 3

As Albert Einstein once said,
There are only two ways to live your life:
As though nothing is a miracle,
Or as though
EVERYTHING is a miracle,
Now he was awakened, connected
and a collector of Empirical.

See spiritualty and science go hand in hand,
Do your research, open your mind,
It's proven in quantum physics multiple times!

An example, think of the radio in your car,
Receiving signals, 'invisible waves', travelling a far.

So what's to say there aren't other waves already in existence?
Un-see able to the untrained eye, but some seen with
persistence.

***

Practice seeing your aura by staring at a candle,
Relax your gaze and after a minute or two look around the
room-
See what your soul is ready to handle.

You may see coloured orbs floating all around,
They may be blue or red or green,
The more you practice, the more will be seen.

Relax your eyes and look around the edges of your hand,
At first you may see a white blur, or other colours- which is grand!

Practice, practice, practice, that's the key point to say,
Connect to your spirit at least once every single day.

After all you're the one you're helping,
You're doing this for you,
And once you care for yourself,
You're better able to help others through.

Remember you are never alone,
But I'm not talking about people ringing up your phone.
I'm talking about you're the Great spirit, your angels and guides,
Your loved ones known in your past and current life,
Supporting you from the 'other side'.

The spiritual world is where they are based,
Rooting for you, hearing your prayers, ready to help you embrace,
Embrace the process of life and let your intuition guide you.

You planned your goals and your journey before you came down,

Connect to this knowledge through your intuition,

Trust me it will all be sound!

You cannot go wrong if you trust your intuition,

Believe in yourself and remember your mission,

Connect with the vision,

And make the decision.

The decision to be kind and love the very special you,

That is the very first thing you need to do.

You were born into this world sparkly eyed, pure heart.

You've been impacted by your experiences and your childhood start.

You've experienced the beauty of this planet- pure art!

Love yourself, the innocent child.

See how amazing you are to have made it up to this day,

Overcoming the challenges that have come your way.

Giving you strength and building you up.

Some may be thinking 'but shit, I've messed up'!

Fear not, as when you decide to make positive change in your
life,

You are supported,

you are forgiven,

all can be put right.

No matter what you have done, or all that you do,

It was an experience necessary that you had to go through.

It is never too late to action good deeds that are due.

Just know your angels and guides love you,

No judgement- it's true.

To connect, just think of them,

Say hello in your head,

Say a prayer in the morning and the evening before bed.

Open your mind to the messages,

Know they are rarely audio hearing,

But take note of signs, songs and things found on your path,

Like a blue butterfly key-ring.

Become aware of sensations you feel in your being.

This is a way to connect with Spirit,

Without using eyes for seeing.

There really is no right or wrong,

You will know yourself as your heart will burst in light and
song.

This is one of those things that's hard to explain to another,

You can only understand it when you experience it yourself,

Like a child birthing mother.

That experience you truly cannot comprehend,

Until you experience it for yourself...

Or any experience for that matter,

Unless you have it on your life experience shelf.

'Spirit message' Part 4

Be kind to yourself.

You are wonderful,

You are unique,

You are special,

You are magical

You have the perfect physique!

The only love you need to win over in life is love for yourself,

After that the rest will come right, all by itself!

Don't base your self-love on productivity, achievements, successes.

No, instead love the awareness inside you, that is reading this now,

The one who experiences all of your challenges and blessings.

This YOU is not your thoughts,

As they come and go.

This YOU is not your emotions,

As they melt away like snow.

This YOU is not 'My body',

That is something that belongs to you,

Just like we say 'my phone', 'my bottle',

Is this understanding getting through?

This YOU is the My, the I,
The one who experiences it all, without having to try.

This YOU is always present here,
Other than when sleeping and you seem to disappear.

That's when you go to dreamland,
But that's a big topic,
We'll cover it another time,
As it won't be quick.

So love the YOU that is the awareness,
Aware of what's going on.
Sit straight,
Feet flat,
Lift up your tongue.

Mouth closed with tongue touching the roof of your mouth,
Relax,
Do your breathing,
Feel the energy moving.

Use your intention to add to life's magic!
Imagine this energy is sparkling, healing your body as travelling it.

Then share this love and positivity to the world,

be valued for generosity,

When connected, our intentions are super powerful,

we each hold the key.

Things are not as they may seem…

We are co-creators in this life dream!

***

Act with love and good intention,

Be creative, get inventing.

The one with the access to our joy, enlightenment and treasure,

Is ourselves if we choose to endeavour.

Despite the situation you find yourself in,

Connect with Spirit, ask for help,

You will be guided from within.

…

Then contentment you will win.

Remember no need to rush,

Everything is in divine timing.

Take action when drawn to do so,

And equally have stillness time within.

'Spirit message' Part 5

The atrocities in the world can be overwhelming.

But succumbing your inner self to fear and anger adds more dark energy to the situation- not helping!

The negativity in the world cannot sink our bodily boat if we don't allow it in,

Then we are able to send good intention and energy,

pray for the world and keep shining.

To keep shining is to stop the darkness from spreading,

Lifting others up instead of doing peoples head in.

One flame can light unlimited candles,

And its flames of light that the dark side can't handle.

To truly rebel against the evil on this planet,

Don't get angry or fearful... express love and let the dark side have it.

Love vs Fear- which one will you spread?

Time to make that important decision in your head.

What you put out into the world,

Becomes your Earth home,

As a collective we are powerful creators,

But we must first begin our journey alone.

Take your time to align.

Trust the wisdom of the Divine.

Relax, don't worry,

Know all will be fine.

What's mine is yours and what's yours is mine.

If not now, this will make sense in time.

The more who awaken, the more the collective will shine.

Think of the power of the light, shining collective,

All viewing and treating the world from a positive perspective.

The manifesting power behind that is so strong,

It can impact our Earth home,

and right all our collective wrongs.

We can create the world of our dreams,

Meditate, envision it, send energy and love,

Work together as a team.

The occupants of the Earth home working together in harmony,

Being aware and connected to the synchronicities.

There is lots we have just covered,

There will be questions I know.

See to which points your Spirit guides you,

Follow your paths flow.

Know you have all your answers already within you,

So Tune in, let go,

Be your true self

and enjoy the show.

***

Mindfulness Meditation

The next poem is about mindfulness meditation- a practice which had a huge influence on my life and pulled me out of an intense depression and anxiety state which I experienced between the ages of 12-19. A community mindfulness meditation group was transformational for me and taught me to let go of past and future whirring thoughts, live in the present moment and see life through a lens of beauty and awe.

I am so grateful to this group and its facilitators for introducing me to this practice and really opening my eyes to what we are capable of and how there is more to this experience to uncover and discover. They taught me that mindfulness involves clearing the mind completely and becoming truly present. Something which I did not realise I wasn't doing, until I actually experienced what it was.

To help get to this state we can focus on things which are present and can only be present. These three things are the sensations in the body, therefore completing a body scan, the breath and the sounds around us. By focusing on these three things, it helps us to become more present, away from thoughts of past and future events. I began doing this practice morning and evening for 20 minutes and was amazed by the results after just two weeks. A new world view and the letting go of depression and anxiety as a side effect of letting go of negative thought patterns. It was a profound and rapid transformation and helped me far more than other things I had tried (like medication which went up to 60mg citalopram age 16, which made me feel like a zombie and detached from myself and my emotions).

Mindfulness meditation helps us to observe our emotions and thoughts without becoming them. To be the witness and allowing them to come, be observed, teach us and then pass.

I fully recommend everyone to try mindfulness meditation as this can be a key part of our self-care toolkit. There are many guided mindfulness meditations you can find online or guide yourself using the techniques mentioned (body scan, breath and sound). Always remember to ground and send energetic roots down into the Earth to give you stability and protection.

Our mind is part of us, but it should not control us. We can work with our mind to serve us for the highest good of all and not create our own inner hell. We can enjoy the experience of being alive, by being present to the life we are living, feeling all the experiences, not just keeping all our energy focused in our head.

Meditation is like an onion- it has many layers. What I have mentioned here is just the beginning. Once the past healing is done and the mind is clear, this is where the inner universe is explored in addition to intention setting and manifestation abilities to influence and create our reality. It is a life time's practice as daily consistency is what offers the most gifts.

Fully feel, fully breath, fully be.

13.'A Lesson on how to 'Be' 19.02.2021

The future is bright!
Trust, have faith, all will be alright!

When the days a struggle, don't give up the fight,
Think positive, be happy, envision what might…
What might be in store, waiting around the corner…
Your dreams come true, healthy planet, everywhere fauna!

Embrace the now,
If you don't know how,
Don't throw in the towel!
Let me guide you a way, make your Spirit howl.

Close your eyes, take a breath,
Let mind and body rest,
Release the stress, try your best,
Feel life's true zest.
Feel your blood running through you,
Follow your breath, the true you!

It is humble yet present all of the time,
It comes and it goes,
Out your mouth, through your nose.
Always there in the background,
Giving you life and connecting you to all around.

The air is the connector between all,
It's within you,
It's around you,
It is everywhere- yes Air!

Air is what claims the space between you and me,
Connecting you to everything, beyond what our eyes see.

As you and I are connected to air, so is EVERYTHING!
Air has no walls or partitions,
Air is but one single thing!

So breathe in this air and know you're connected.
...
Now you are ready to move on to the next bit...
Life is so much more than expected!

Take your awareness now to your ear,
Listen to sounds that are far...
Now listen to sounds that are near.
Relax, focus- you're doing fine dear!

Can you hear birds? Traffic? Your breathing?
Can you hear people walking, talking, laughing, sneezing?
This dark world of sound you now find yourself in,
Takes your awareness further than the room you are in.

A true example that your being, your awareness,
is more than you see...
Mind-blowing I know,
when you realise you are more than just a physical body.

When you focus on your sensations,
not just what's in your head,
To the true experience of life you will be led.
You can do this in nature, on a train, in your bed.
You can do this all the time,
let your awareness spread!

Connect above and below,
good intentions, open heart,
once connected you'll know!

Send your roots deep down with our Earth Mother.
Send a light beam up your spine to Father Sky.
To keep you grounded, yet uplifted, not just one or the other.

Must be balanced to keep you stable,

As this will enable – you

To be present here on Earth,

but connect to the far stars too.

So send down your connecting Earth roots,

It's best to remove your shoes, socks, boots.

Then imagine a light thread,

from your head,

connecting you above the sky,

you are an energy channel between the two,

you, them, trees and I-

when you feel the presence of Spirit,

don't be shy,

say hi!

Don't try to figure out how or why,

Just experience for yourself and think oh my!

But stay relaxed, no expectations, it's best not to try.

As when we relax and let go that's when it happens,

Waves of tingly warm feelings- no you don't need a statin!

Feel for yourself, the love the feeling brings,

It can feel magnetic, heavy, uplifting,

It can make your heart sing.

The Great Spirit has you, under its wing,

Peace, love and abundance this will bring!

So you receive so much, that now you must give.

The energy exchange circle,

So energy not lost through a sieve.

We are channels connecting Earth and Sky,

Felt most when we are a clean vessel,

so limit poisons we must try.

Feel Earth and Sky energies connecting at your heart,

in golden light.

Use your intention and imagination to start

and soon you will feel the delight.

Then expand this golden light from your heart centre,

Using your breath to expand it around you,

like a placenta!

Put in your intentions of peace, health and connection,

This bubble of light will give you strength, joy and protection.

Using intention, you can expand this light further if you wish,

Your imagination is limitless-

you can encompass the whole world in bliss!

Let the energy come and go,

With our breath it will flow.

Breathe energy up our spine,

pulling up our root,

Send it to the top of our head,

hold for a second like a rising shoot.

Breath out and push the energy down to the belly (lower Dantien)

Our energy centre, energy stored here,

a yin yang balanced blend.

The 'microcosmic orbit' this is called

(Mantak Chia-The Tao)

Helps keep energy flowing and cycling within,

why not try it now?

Energy is always abundant, never running out.

This applies also to our daily external lives without a doubt.

To keep the energy exchange circle tight and flowing,

with everyone and all of this planet,

we must be knowing,

To receive ourselves as well as give,

To take care of ourselves,

as we do the kids.

To keep the circle flowing, we must do both,

To yourself make the Oath.

Do it with love,

Keep aware, connect above.
Be present, learn lessons,
Be chill, no stressing.

So there you have it,
that's the end of this lesson,
Now your own journey you shall continue,
or begin.

***

Remember we are not the emotions as they come and go, yet we remain. We are merely the witness, the energy, the being, experiencing it all. The way to release emotions is to allow them be felt, dealt with, healed, and then they can melt away. From there we can learn the lessons which support our strength and transformation, helping us to navigate our path through this current life.

Also, try not to succumb to shutting down emotionally and bottling them up inside never to be felt. Eventually this method can manifest as illness and disease. Crying is a way to release the trapped emotions and is a strength; it is the body's ability to cleanse emotionally, to sustain good health. A superpower in that sense. Not to be mistaken for weakness.

I feel intensely in the moment, but I do not hold on to bad experiences. The quicker I can process, heal, and forgive myself and others, the better I feel in the present moment and can then feel and share that love. See the lessons or the humans within the experience, knowing that everyone is on different journeys with their own reasons for their actions.

14.'The Silver Lining' 20.02.2021

Almost a year in lockdown,
The world in shutdown!

Times like these not seen before…
A weird experience, that's for sure.

Unable to visit friends or family,
Unless you meet at 2m distance under a tree.

There are pros and cons as with all things.
Less traffic pollution is a highlight,
but sad not to meet friends and sing.

Some people have passed away,
Some people have sobbed,
Some people have lost jobs,
Some people feel their freedom is robbed.

But there are some positives in all this dark.
Time for reflection, nature time in the park.

The whole world experiencing the 'Winter' of the Earth.

Being quiet, reflecting, able to envision a new planet to birth.

For when the Earth's 'Spring' comes,

The preparation will be done!

Astrologists know this as the 'Golden age', a new era,

The age of Aquarius!

Our Earth's saviour.

A new way of thinking and working with,

not against,

Our dear Mother Nature,

Oh the suspense!

These times now offer the space to retreat,

Into ourselves, from our head to our feet.

The treasures that await when you look deep inside,

You with yourself, nowhere to hide.

All the negative stories and emotions repressed,

Come now to the surface, to be expressed.

But these must be embraced, they are growing pains.

Experience and release, again and again.

Once you have cleared all those dark clouds,

You'll make way for Spirit to speak clear and loud.

Once connected with Spirit, everything is okay,
No stress, no worries, Spirit guides the way.

Once peace within,
there's no need to look externally,
For the world around you,
to feed your happiness eternally.
To go within and find happiness ourselves,
means we have to look no longer,
out in the worlds shelves.

Externally there are so many factors impacting our happiness,
The peace feeling is never stable,
So therefore we will miss-
The present moment and all sensational experience,
As we're always chasing the dragon of happiness,
Making us tired and serious.

But once peace is found within it cannot be taken or disturbed,
It is a loving song inside of you,
that always can be heard.

So no longer do you need to chase the 'happiness dragon',
Giving you freedom to jump off the high-speed wagon!
Then down you roll into a wildflower meadow…
You have now made peace with your shadow.

You don't need to let external events into your peace bubble.
Envision a bright strong colour, surrounding you-
a protective love cuddle.

Love and strength is what you need
if you want to succeed.
Protect your peace at all costs-
Do it with love and it won't be lost.

Now is your chance,
You can do it if you try,
You can do it, you can fly!
This is the silver lining of the current situation,
Our opportunity to reduce internal and external hating.
Expand your light bubble,
Bigger with intention, no trouble.

Expand bit by bit, start with your house and family,
Your local area, your state, your whole country!
Intend it bigger and bigger, until the whole Earth you surround,
Send love from within, flowing in abundance, all around.

You are expansive, you are power,
You are connected, a radiant flower!

Be sure to ground, sending roots down into the Earth beneath you.

Share your good intentions with the planet, each country and the universe as a whole too.

Be open to Spirit, this light comes from within.

And use your breath to help the energy spin!

So the 'Winter' of our planet,

You have well spent,

Ready now to let the external battle for peace commence.

The next poem was inspired by a message from a movie I watched as a child and the message was strong. The movie is called ANTZ and at the very end of the film, after having insight into the life of ants and their whole kingdom and personalities etc. the camera zooms out and you realise that the whole movie was based near a bin in a big park in somewhere like New York, yet the Ants had no perception that they were part of something so much bigger.

Who is to say that we are not living in a similar reality, unaware that we are part of something so vast that we cannot comprehend it?

15. 'Zooming in and Zooming out' 21.02.2021

If you go down to the woods today,
You very well might just see,
A girl in blue, sat on a rock,
Leaning against a tall pine tree.
She may be writing or doing Qi Gong,
And yes, that girl is me.
A black and white dog,
Prancing around, as joyous as can be,
Present and joyful,
Fluffy, loving and kind,
my boy, sweet, Kody.
Both are connected, hearts are one,
exploring life with curiosity.

Mother Nature is the ultimate healer,
Taking away your troubles, if you allow her and feel her.

Use your senses,
Notice the colours and textures,
The sounds and smells, and all the extras!

Become still spectators,
Do it now and later,
Quiet your mind, be open,
Marvel at the creator.

The creator that encompasses you and I,
The creator that encompasses soil, plants, sunsets
and birds in the sky.

We are in it, we are part of it,
Now that's just the start of it!
As if we are in it, we must be a star in it.
That's right you can go really far with this,
If you grasp your true part in this.

***

To help understand, think of micro-organisms,
They are found everywhere- soil, air, water,
In your guts and kitchen sinks.
Micro means tiny,
Organism means creature that's living.
Some are harmful to us
And some are giving.

Now apply that concept to people,
You can see how they are equal.

To us micro-organisms are tiny and small,
But to them we are big and we are tall.

But they may not even be aware of us,
Too big to comprehend and thus
They may just go about their life's as we do,
Unaware that what they are part of is much bigger than mud on
a human shoe.

Now let's apply that same theory to us,
That we are part of something bigger, lets discuss!
This may sound scary, but trust, it's a plus
Open the borders of our mind- that is a must.

Zoom out, know that life is bigger than just our career.
Ask the scary question
'what am I doing here?'.

We know we live on a planet,
rotating around the Sun,
Part of a universe which is expansive, maybe infinite,
and there's more than one!

Just like the micro-organisms living in our body,
We may be part of something too big for us to comprehend...
Use imagination, then curiosity and magic we can embody!

As a human we will never know for sure…
That's okay as the teaching is to live life in awe!

Like a parachute, your mind only works when it's open,
Listen to the truths that are too often unspoken,
Blindfolds and spells of lies must be broken…
Writing this I'm choking,
Laughing to myself,
As all the words to describe the truth,
Society has stacked on the 'looney' shelf.
For example words like 'love', 'light', and 'magic',
Mainstream mind sets have labelled as 'fluffy' or 'dramatic'.

T.V, schools, the government and the media,
'Educating us', yet main truths of life not on the criteria.

Yes many of them do know it,
But they will not show it–
As if they did that, everyone would be happy, peaceful, free,
Therefore no one would be a slave to the system,
chasing money.

We did not come to this Earth to focus all our energy on paying
bills and taxes,
We came to experience, to love, to learn skills and cool tricks.

Take away the money, you take away the power,
and then life's' true riches will shower.

Not isolated in our homes,
but living together as a collective,
Together growing food, exchanging skills,
in every way connected.

Loving thy neighbour as myself can truly be applied,
Relax, no fear, all will be supplied,
As you're part of Earths tribe.

Everyone contributing in the ways they are able,
So many good intentions that the system is stable.
Everything provided for all, no need for money,
Those less able offer wisdom, understanding, a cup of tea.
All are cared for in the Earth tribe family.

With time caring for others widely distributed,
People caring for family and the less able,
Have their responsibilities diluted,
This means feelings of depravity and being drained are muted,
Respect and compassion, everyone is saluted.

Now these once full-time carers can have time to self-
their own dreams, let's do this!

Increasing quality of life for everyone-
This way everyone can be included!
For experiencing the joys in life no one should be excluded.

For this shift, let's prepare,
Metaphorically get suited and booted!
To change our ways, a lot must be done,
To free ourselves and change the future outcome.

It's okay, we can do it, we are not alone,
A single grain of sand multiplied can become a huge strong sandstone.

When we pull together, we make change happen,
If we each of us do it, we make up for those slacking.
So let's get cracking,
It's happening,
The collective is now crackling,
And the embers setting fire to the shackling's.
The shackling's of old ways snapping and crumbling,
The thunder in our hearts, lightning and rumbling.

When good intentions pull together,
it sends the evil things tumbling.
To do this you must connect with the pure Spirit of your heart,
The pure you who came to Earth as a baby at the start.

Once aligned with truth, love for all, good intentions,
You are the ultimate invention!
A magnet of light,
a disperser of tension.

Spread compassion and affection,
What you give out you receive-
the Earth is your reflection.

Oh and did I mention,
to realise this is part of your ascension!
On your journey to be freed from all the deception,
Giving you space to re-focus your attention.

It's right to be full of apprehension,
As all of what I speak is not the convention.
But trust that's it's a therapeutic intervention!
No feelings of condescension,
Just compassion, magic and seeing a new dimension.

What's holding you back? That is the question.
As a tribe there's no need to worry about your pension!
Our true human nature is sentient,
Taking care of one and all, the baby, the gran, the henchman.

Working together we can reach close to perfection,
So climb aboard the peace ship, take a seat, start the engine.

16.'Positive affirmation Power' 13.03.2021

It's so funny I remember writing this one imagining having a microphone on the streets of London and doing this to encourage strangers to connect, lift people up and decrease the feeling of being alone.

I then had a dream that me and Stormzy became really good friends and he liked my expressions lol.

***

So right now let's discuss positive affirmation,
This can be influential enough to change oneself
and each and every nation.

Our thoughts impact our behaviour,
They can be our downfall or our saviour.
So choose wisely your thought flavour,
Knowing what's at stake here.

Our internal universe reflects our external,
A mirror...
Just the same as the external universe reflects our internal...
It's a never-ending circle.

The external world we cannot control,

Trying to do so burns us out, damages our soul.

Yet the internal universe,

We are the overall creator,

So we can nourish and love the universe within us,

Or we can be a hater.

This is the universe where we hold the reins,

We are the director, the leader,

We can control our gains,

With help from our brains.

Our brains can be destructive and cause pain,

Or they can be our golden tool,

With which life's treasures we can gain.

Strength in seeing silver linings we must obtain...

Let me explain...

Life has good and bad, there is sunshine, then it rains.

Feel all that you feel, embrace it, but do not hold this low emotion in chains.

You can release it, let go, it doesn't need to remain.

Then you have space to claim,

The gratitude for each present moment,

Marvelling at life, look around- keep your mind open.

Look at the sky, always moving, colour changing work of art,

Look at the plants, the animals- this creation is smart!

We can feel gratitude for that even if nothing else,

Marvel at this moment…

You are ALIVE.

So join in with me,

You can say it out loud, or internally,

Look in the mirror or to another,

lock eyes and discover,

The gratitude within

for this amazing being.

Stood before you,

you don't need to know them to know they are a work of art too.

Now repeat after me, aloud or inside,

No need to be shy and hide,

Join in this experience to feel fully alive.

Positive affirmations we now send to this person, repeat after me:

"I respect you, I value you, I see your inner light,

Let me tell you, you are strong, you are wonderful, you shine so bright!

You are brave, you are kind,
You are unique, a beautiful mind.

You are a human living in the same game as me,
I respect you, I see you, together let's live free
I send you positivity and good luck on your journey.

Good luck for your challenges and your soul's learning,
I believe in you, you got this, keep your fire of love and passion
inside burning".

***

Now let's address ourselves in this same manner,
We are deserving of our love too,
Gear up self-respect with our mind spanner.

Repeat these words and re-wire,
Let's lift ourselves higher, admire, inspire!
"I am loving, I am strong,
I am with me lifelong.
I am brave and I am beautiful,
Like sweet bird song.
I've got through all challenges,
I've embraced all my scars.
I made it this far,
I am here, what a star!

I am grateful, I am excited,
My inner fire I have lighted!"

***

You have now been consciously knighted,
The divine is delighted.
So now let's pull our light together,
humanity and Earth, one and all- united.

17.'Babbling Brook: Brothers and Sisters of the Earth' 15.03.2021

Bare foot in the stream,

Feel like I'm in a dream,

In the fairy woodland, with the fairy woodland team.

Towering trees,

Babbling brook,

So much magic when I look.

Looking at the details, textures, colours, sounds,

So many beings, so many lives,

surrounding me all around.

Each going about their unique existence,

But all coming together, forming the magic systems.

The systems that connect everything and everyone in the flow,

To be separate from nature is suffering,

so join the natural system- let go!

Let go and you'll know,

You are a part of this world, not just a visitor- oh no.

We are all mammals, we fit the criteria,
Same as the animals, plants and bacteria,
Oh the hysteria!

So you see, we are all accepted and belong,
We are part of the Earth.
We become part of this planet the day our mum's gave birth!

No need for racism or hierarchy's- that sh*t's absurd,
We are all valuable, so respect others- spread the word!
And I mean this with depth,
Every being deserves respect.
Especially those who society has under the rug swept.

Shout out to the beings who have disabilities.
Shout out to beings with different abilities.
Should out to the beings who have travelled from overseas.
Shout out to the beings of all nationalities.
Shout out to the beings who have no house keys.
Shout out the beings whose 'pure purpose' is to 'feed'.
So be kind and spread respect and love, please.

Shout out to those who follow different religions,
And let's please embrace the fact they all share the same origins.
Allah, God, Divine, Great Spirit- are all names used for source,
The overall creator and provider of all resource.

All Religions have compassion as a core element,

This should be concrete in religious practice and in life-

pure cement.

The details and differences are down to culture and those in

power throughout time,

And be aware there have been different control agendas

throughout the human race's timeline.

Each individuals chosen path to the divine should be respected,

However, any violence 'in the name of God' must be neglected

and rejected.

There is no right or wrong route to spirituality when

compassion is the driving force for our actions.

To connect with the creator is available for all to access.

You can be guided by religion,

or you can make your own practice,

But remember all you seek is within you,

be wary of religious or spiritual malpractice.

There are some evil tactics,

Which at first can seem attractive,

But it can spike you like a cactus,

And bring nothing but darkness and keep you distracted.

Shout out to the females- one powerful sisterhood!

Shout out to the males- one protective brotherhood!

Shout out the LGBTQ community and those who do not align to one single gender,

I see you, I include you, the message conveyed in the next lines is for you too.

We have lots to learn from our opposite gender,

To balance male and female energies within ourselves is on our life's agenda.

Be open to the knowledge, both and all sides surrender.

Both with good intentions and respect- be tender.

That same applies to all you meet,

You have lessons to learn from everyone- all are unique.

Open your mind to people you may think have nothing to teach,

Remember learning doesn't have to be through words and speech.

Put yourself in the others shoes,

Value them, connect,

There is nothing to lose…

Yet so much to gain!

Your words or acknowledgment could make someone's day!

A nice gesture or smile goes such a long way.

The game of life gets better when this way you play.

So get yourself down to a babbling brook,

dip your toes in,

Indulge in the fact you are not a separate thing,

Not an isolated being.

Connect with yourself,

others and the Earth's magic systems.

This is how this life game you will enjoy and metaphorically win.

18.'The Universe and planets' 16.03.2021

Zoom out and remember the madness of it all,

A planet floating around in space-

and that's just a short summary of this miracle!

To understand what I am saying,

You don't need to be considered spiritual,

It's a vast topic so I will summarise it through words that are lyrical.

We live on a round spinning mass,

Comprised of land, sea and skies,

This is a wonder in itself- no surprise,

use your eyes!

Consider the intelligence of the transformation of butterflies.

Listen to the broad range of bird cries.

These are wonders in themselves,

all truth, no lies.

Zoom out again and be aware that our planet is circling,

Our bright Sun, giver of life and energy for certain.

This giant mass of fire,

Let's admire.

It's the start point of all life,

feeding the plant choir,

Which in turn makes it habitable for us to live and retire.

The sun provides us heat and energy,

It can make us perspire.

Now this ball of fire is nearly 150 million KM away,

So imagine its power up close,

when you're sat in the heat of midday.

Now let's bring our attention to the beautiful Moon,

Seen in the sky at night like a shining balloon.

When we look up at the Moon,

know we are all looking at the same,

There is only one Moon we can see from this planet of the life game.

Allow this knowing to help you feel connected to others around the world,

All marvelling at our wondrous Moon, aware too that it twirls.

This twirling Moon causes cycles on our dear planet,

It impacts the oceans, pulling tide in and out.

It impacts all beings and humans too-

The human body is averaged 60% water- that's a big clue!

We can 'prove' with science the impact the Moon has on water,
So we too should be aware it must impact ourselves,
sons, daughters.

All of us are sons or daughters of this Earth, beloved Mother,
And our beloved Father Sky,
who nourish us to support everything- and each other!
Our Moon that impacts all life so greatly,
Is approximately 385,000Km away- science announced lately.

Zoom out again, be aware of our entire solar system,
8 planets with different properties and powers,
I'm not kidding!
Neptune affects our aspirations and dreams.
Uranus represents change so it seems.
Venus rules love and relationships.
Saturn represents challenges and where we may trip.
Mars affects our deep primal energy,
It impacts our instincts, aggression and sexuality.
Beneath Pluto's gaze, secrets unfold,
Inner realms revealed, a story untold …
Mercury rules thinking, expression and communication.
Jupiter impacts our fortune and higher learning
for our Earth Nation.
You see there are many layers to this marvellous creation.
Check out your full birth chart to have insight into what I am
saying.

Zoom out again and be aware we are in the Milky Way galaxy,

Formed of at least 100 billion stars,

Each with their own present and ancestry.

Science estimates it would take 100,000 light years to cross from side to side,

Yeah seriously, it's really fricken wide!

Zoom out again and be aware the Milky Way is in a cluster of at least 40 other galaxies!

I guess we will never know for sure...

Keep minds open please.

The zooming out could be endless for all that we know,

But wow to be part of something so big is astounding- no?!

Let's draw our awareness back now to our individual perspective,

Knowing we all belong to something bigger,

part of the collective.

When life gets too much, and anxiety creeps,

Try this zoom out technique,

And allow the miracle of everything to present to you

and speak.

Another year of progress and process

After leaving work at the mental health hospital and moving back home, it took me a year before I wrote another poem. During that time, a lot happened.

As mentioned, I had left work to dedicate my time to recording Jim's Qi Gong style and wanted to share some levels on YouTube to benefit everyone's health and wellbeing. However, I got stuck on the technical side. I wanted to add a voiceover, music, and written instructions to cater to all learning styles, but I became overwhelmed and unsure where to start. My self-doubt increased, and I found myself in a dark place.

I decided to return to part-time occupational therapy, a field that fulfils me. I began working at a children's charity for autism diagnosis and sensory/functional occupational therapy assessments, four days a week. Joining a big team after a long period of isolation was initially overwhelming.

The role was specialised, so there was a lot to learn. On my days off, I sought new adventures to boost my mental health, such as chasing waterfalls in Wales and wild swimming (Sagittarius moon in me). Consequently, my projects were put on hold.

Working in Autism diagnosis and OT intervention for three years was fascinating and gave me a deep and wide insight. Learning about the indicators, I realised that many of these behaviours seemed normal to me. This led to the revelation that I matched the criteria for what used to be known as Autism Asperger's, confirmed by the multi-disciplinary team I worked with who saw this in me too. I remembered being briefly tested for this in school, but it was dismissed after a short screening, which concluded I had an interesting way of thinking and creative mind, but went no further. At university, my learning challenges led to a dyslexia assessment, which revealed no dyslexia, but slow audio processing skills—another autism indicator, as I later learnt. Jim had also noted my black-and-white thinking, suggesting my brain worked in a way that is classed as 'Autistic', though he advised against getting attached to a label as every human is uniquely different and wonderful as they are and do not need to be put inside a labelled box.

Understanding these similarities has been enlightening, helping me learn new strategies to manage better. Interestingly, I seem to have a radar for other Autistic/ ADHD people, finding it easiest to connect and communicate with them.

The next poem I think fits best here.

It is an insight into some of my experience.

Everyone's experience of Autism is different as it is a wide spectrum.

I am learning more about Autism all the time... see the last point of the self-care toolkit in the appendix to see what I am currently exploring!

19.'Autism' 05.12.2022

Black and white thinking.
Loves repetition.
Sensory differences.
Appears on a mission.

Vulnerable socially.
The 'gullible' definition.
Take things literally.
Hard to regulate emotions.

A person of extremes,
Reckless at times it seems.
Says it how it is, no filter
Pure honesty
But sometimes the truth will kill ya.

Seen by some as a weirdo,
But positively unique once you know.
Extreme interests,
can be obsessed.
Intense in everyway
Can be super chill or super stressed.

An unusual thought process,

often think in pictures,

Amazing memory for what takes my interest,

Could be song lyrics, phone numbers, or ancient scriptures.

Other time memory seems poor, very different,

I often live very engrossed in the present.

Other times my head is spinning, full of ideas...

Can become overwhelmed and stagnated in dysregulation and tears.

Take on too much, feeling positive to do it all,

But sometimes it's too much,

and that's when I may fall.

What is this grey area that people mention?

To me it's all or nothing,

The go hard or go home dimension.

Could be an alcoholic, or could be tee-total,

Can eat 10 chocolate bars at once, or a salad with tofu.

Each decision can be crippling,

As the outcome appears to be one of two things,

First- it could be a miracle!

Second it could be the end of me and everything

- no next sequel.

Hard to adapt to sudden change,
This shakes the world and seems strange.

Likes to know the social rules,
The ones not taught in schools.
What to expect, what is the plan,
what do I need to bring if I can.
Love making daily lists,
That feeling of satisfaction that comes with each tick,
If not written down I will forget it quick.

Routines and rituals, can seem very habitual,
But also loves risks and the spontaneity of it all...
May appear contradictory,
But in my mind it's balanced, do you see?

So humans have called this presentation 'ASD',
But it could also just be called 'personality'
As all of the above is written in my star birth chart of me.

Autism is a spectrum,
Impacts each a different way,
As we know, no two people are the same.
For some it can be very challenging and inhibiting,
Impacting ability to function in daily living.
Interventions and support can be required,
for increased quality of life bringing in.

For others it's a positive and facilitates them to better change the world we are in,

As an Autistic mind is unique,

So unique ideas it can bring.

***

Some of my Autistic traits can lead me to taking risks (not seeing the danger, mixing up red and green flags, trusting that everyone tells the truth (turns out they don't!)… some of these instances lead onto an amazing experience, and some not so much.

I have had some amazing and wild experiences, guided by the Sagittarius moon in me. Some risky, some naïve and some close calls too.

One core memory that comes to mind is when I slipped down a big waterfall in Thailand mountains when I was 21 (2018). It was an epic fall and I smashed against rocks twice, yet I somehow remained floppy and only ending up with a slight bruise on my cheek and my elbow, despite my face slamming into a big rock as I was carried by the rushing water down to the next level, where I hit another huge rock.

I was a bit stunned, and teenage and child monks with orange robes came to me asking "bones broken?" as signalling to my arms and collar bones. I stood up and checked myself. I was lucky and surprisingly okay, and survived the dramatic fall with just a few scrapes and bruises. I thought "thank you God" and gave the monks a smile and a thumbs up "all okay I think".

They then invited me and Kirsty to play with them on the 'natural waterslide' smooth rock, which we did with glee. We connected through play, gestures and eye contact and although this could have gone badly, the falling down the waterfall ended up as a core memory. The monks were also doing mad flips from the top of a tree which was on top of a huge rock, jumping from some 10-15m into the small but deep pool below. Their skills were phenomenal. They scaled up the tree trunk like on Mulan. Their fitness, balance and skills intrigued and inspired me greatly.

It was actually seeing them jumping and swimming from where we were (further up the mountain) which inspired us to try to get to the part of the water fall they were at in the first place. Where we were to begin with, there were signs that said "Danger- no swimming", which we were gutted by, as the main reason we climbed the mountain was with the hope of swimming in the waterfall!

We thought where the monks were must be safe for swimming, if they were swimming (in hindsight I don't think it was safe, I just think they are good swimmers and can handle it). Anyhow, to get down to them we thought it was a good idea (at the time) to scale down a huge round rock face boulder half sitting, half walking on hands and feet. Here, one of my feet went onto a wet part of the boulder and I slipped, and that's how this event began.

The Duality

In summer (2021), age 24, I attended a conscious community spiritual event and there I met a member of the black jaguar tribe; his name is Tlilik Tekuani (meaning 'Black Jaguar'). He is a crazy, powerful soul from Mexico. We became friends and initially communicated through our eyes and actions, especially while doing Qi Gong by the lake during the full moon, as his English was limited and my Spanish was nearly non-existent. He calls me his duality. While he loves the darkness, the underworld, and skulls, I am drawn to the light, unicorns, angels, and rainbows. He taught me not to fear the darkness because, in its depths, there can be love. Not all things 'dark' are 'evil'; evil is in its own category. Tlilik Tekuani has indigenous roots and connections and often pushes me out of my comfort zone, which, though sometimes painful, helps me develop and learn.

Tlilik Tekuani is a beautiful example of this duality. He follows Mayan traditions and is deeply connected to the darker aspects of spirituality, yet he is one of the most peaceful, open, and loving humans I have ever met. He holds no judgments and embraces everyone with love. Tlilik Tekuani has his missions to change the world, raise its frequency, and help consciousness transform and expand. He is a powerful musician, performing unique sound journeys. He also helps people birth their own shamanic drum from ethically and sustainably sourced materials. This process is a ceremony, connecting with the spirit of the animal, offering respect and expansion of its being, continuing its heartbeat through the drum. Tlilik Tekuani also facilitates voice activation workshops. His work with frequency and vibration heals the body, mind, and spirit, through making sounds which resonate with the Earth, Sky, around us, our creative centre and to expand out into the world with love. The vibrations these sounds make within our body bring great healing.

20.   'Duality' 12.10.2021

My duality,

Is the opposite of me,

So different yet so similar,

Which is quite mesmerising.

I like unicorns,

He likes devil horns,

I like the light,

He likes the dark,

I like to be bright,

And he too likes a laugh.

He is not all darkness,

Like I am not all light,

There is Yin within Yang

And Yang within Yin,

And accepting we are both is the delight!

We are mirrors,

We are triggers,

We are lessons,

We are healers,

We have a beautiful connection,

Strong bond, deep friendship,

We will always be there for each other,

Super team,

Supportive companionship and

Supporting each other's dreams.

Tlilik Tekuani also directed me to groups around the world where I could further explore spiritual ceremonies with fire and plant allies. These experiences have been mind-blowing and transformational—like, WOAH!

I had a master medicine experience with a medicine carrier of the Otac (also known as Bufo, a form of 5-MEO-DMT) who I met during my travels. This compound, released when we are born and when we die, helps us cross over into the spiritual world. This experience was unbelievably beautiful and expansive!

Jim always told me I did not need to work with these medicine teachers, as he could teach me how to reach these experiences without external input. I promised myself I would not seek these things out, but when the opportunities landed in my lap and felt right, I knew this was my next step, especially since Jim is no longer here in person to guide me.

Engaging with plant and master medicines took my experience and perspective of life to a new level. I learnt the power of ceremony, preparation, intention, and respect when working with such teachers. I have become healthier and more willing to acknowledge and embrace my own shadow. The medicines I have worked with include Otac, Kambo, Hape, Ayahuasca and Magic mushrooms. They have given me deep insight, understanding, release, and healing. I am deeply grateful.

What amazes me is how many master medicines exist and their potential for healing, though this is not mainstream knowledge. Working with these medicines in ceremonies with intention and respect has been extremely vision-opening and healing. They are keys to healing the deepest parts of the self and offer profound insight and wisdom. A single ceremony can change your life.

If you feel called to explore this path, I encourage you to find a guide or space holder to ensure your safety. These medicines should be used mindfully, respectfully and with intention, including preparation work beforehand and integration work afterwards. Extra care is needed for those with pre-existing health conditions, and some medications or health conditions are dangerous when mixed with master medicines. It is crucial to understand all of this and discuss it with a facilitator and your doctor, if you do wish to explore these natural, ancient medicines.

It is also advisable to prepare the body by eating clean, abstaining from alcohol and hard drugs, and limiting coffee and sugar intake. The cleaner the vessel, the cleaner the experience. In addition, long term preparation by daily meditation practice, cleansing the spirit and mind and time in nature is important. To provide some insight, there are key things to be done to be safe during engagement with such medicines, which I have summarised in the next poem.

21.'Master Medicines' 04.12.2022

Open my eyes, all three,
The magic of this universe let me see.
Heal my emotions and blockages
From them set me free.

Cleanse my spirit pure, allow me to be.
To be healed, transformed,
My mind no longer conformed,
My disillusioned version of 'reality' torn
My spirit into this world re-born.

Master medicines, beautiful teachers,
Thank you, Mother Earth, for providing these guides
in unlocking life's secrets.
Our healing and our mission they are guiding,
Can save us from the dark hole in which we are sliding,
Bringing together knowledge and transformation colliding,

To create the alchemy of wisdom-
My heart they have won.
Integration after lessons is always to be done,
So the gifts and learnings do not come undone.

Intention is everything so ceremony is essential,

Can be done alone or in a group,

Just know that setting clear intentions is very influential.

Cleanse the body, mind, spirit and space,

Meditate, Qi gong, smudging,

and love in your heart embrace.

Take your time with this, there is no race.

First give thanks and show your appreciation,

To the four directions, the Earth, the Sky, the centre

and all of creation.

Say it from your heart,

give an offering and feel the emotion,

Ask for protection and learning

and then set the healing in motion.

Show respect always for the spirit of the medicines,

For all wisdom carriers and ancestors,

For the space where you are and all beings and spirits within.

Once the above is done, consume the medicine with open heart,

Relax, surrender, be curious,

The alteration of the senses will begin to start.

Keep open but strong in spirit,

Request angel help if you need it.

Embrace the journey,

For this your spirit has been yearning,

Savour the experience and all its learnings.

Life is not the same once an alternate reality has shown you
your wings.

You may want to laugh, cry, puke or sing.

You may want to go internal

or externally express your being.

You will come face to face with your own darkness,

You can scream, be in fear, cry or transmute it through laughter.

Once faced it has less power over us,

So embrace it with love and it will dissolve, please trust.

Those emotions locked inside us for years,

Now able to be released from the body through tears.

Past traumas and troubles can be worked through,

Cut through the chains they have been holding over you.

Then you are free to explore the medicines- intention of
curiosity,

Once past healing is done,

you can look deeper into life's mysteries.

A greater insight into this great complexity,

Understood by using the mind set of simplicity.

They may teach you how to communicate with the trees,

Or to meditate with animals like hummingbirds and bees.

They may show you visions or the cosmic web,

They may show you the true rhythm of flow and eb.

So trust and let your spirit be led.

You will always have the experience that is right for you at the time,

So accept it, embrace it and be humble,

keeping this in mind.

Use the power of your breath to breathe deeply into

your 'lower dantian' energy centre,

gather your energy to feel grounded and stable

before, during and after your adventure.

When the journey is over and you're back in the usual dimension,

Remember to express thanks once again to all beings, spirits and the directions.

Close the directions by thanking them, closing the portal,

This is super important, if not done can be dangerous,

may be energetically fatal.

But importantly...

Don't rely on master medicines

for all the answers and solutions,

There are other ways for healing,

be clear on that, no confusions.

Don't believe 'only the medicine path works for everybody' illusions.

They just help facilitate opening what's already within us.

Only engage with them following intuition,

careful not to excess.

Putting in the work through your own daily practices

you must accept.

Integrate what you've learned, don't neglect.

If you need clarity, ask- be clear and direct.

Thank you to all the beings who have kept the ceremony alive,

Allowing the ultimate medicine wisdom to survive,

If we can share and spread this knowledge,

it's the masses that can thrive.

The experiences can be profound and offer insights into life beyond our human form. However, it is important to stay present, to this current life we are living, as we are here to have the human experience. These moments remind us that this is just one chapter in our soul's book of existence. To make the most of each chapter, we must remain present and strive to be kind to ourselves and the world. We can positively impact our inner selves and those we encounter, spreading smiles and love.

Some things cannot be explained by the human mind, as our brains are smaller than the creators. The mystery is part of the joy and fuels our curiosity, much like we see in children. Unfortunately, our society often suppresses this curiosity and diminishes many people's belief in the magnificence of it all. We exist to be free and transform, not merely to pay taxes and be stressed as central aspects of living. Life will knock us down numerous times, but we can always choose to rise again. The important point is to always rise, no matter how many times we fall.

We must embrace the feeling of the low, meditate, and truly feel it. Be curious about the experience of the emotion, but do not become it. Remain the observer—the soul within, experiencing life in all its dark and light forms.

For me, when I engaged with the medicine, it confirmed what I already believed, providing both comfort and curiosity. Having foundational practices like meditation, Qi Gong, and gratitude in my daily routine for years before this experience allowed me greater control over my mind, body, and energy. I advise anyone interested in these master medicines to first establish a solid foundation of spiritual strengthening practices. Discover what works for you and incorporate it into your daily routine. Make it achievable and enjoyable. These foundational blocks will support your process and help you integrate the experience and wisdom into your daily life. This is the safest way to engage. And remember, it is also possible to reach such states through consistent deep meditation practices.

The Assignment

A new man started at Kung fu class. He is a magician but an ACTUAL magician, they are not tricks, it is actually magic. He is part of the magic circle, which is very secretive, and he is very spiritual and psychic, and maybe not of this Earth. On the first night I met him I went in a partner with him to do Kung fu. He is a black sash and the kung fu that he knows is next level! I also noticed his eyes… a deep brown and I can see the strength of his soul in them, so powerful, mystical, strong and deep. I know those eyes have seen some things. The eyes are the windows to the soul. Already, I was intrigued.

He shared with me some interesting things... including that he had been assigned by his spirit guides to find me and to continue teaching me self-defence, carrying on from Jim. This was all very peculiar and at the time I believed him fully and was perhaps somewhat naive, trusting openly that Jim had sent him to me from Spirit to continue my training. He said he teaches 1:1 self-defence and asked would I like some training before my first solo travel to Greece. I was super excited by this and grateful for this offer and I accepted.

22.   'The Magician' 30.12.2022

Well, what a mad one.
I must be a mad one!
The excitement has taken away my sad one,
And turned my face expression into a glad one.

A new teacher to guide me and continue my learning,
For this input I have been subconsciously yearning,
It feels part of the bigger plan, the planet keeps turning,
Time to strengthen my physical, bones strong like sterling.

What are the odds,
A magician come to teach me,
The art of Kung Fu and self-defence,
To deepen my knowledge of Qi Gong and healing.

Very similar to me, a Scorpio ascendant;
mysterious, magical, intuitive and sensitive.
I find him intriguing,
I know he is wise,
I am grateful to have crossed paths with him in this life.

Sent by the guides and angels,
He says I need protecting,
But that I must learn to do this for myself,
Independent, capable and good at reflecting.

Reflecting any danger that comes my way,
Avoiding it using thoughts, then words,
But also feeling confident to defend myself,
knowing my own worth.

I am excited, I am grateful,
I will see where this takes me,
I am ready to embrace this experience
and commit to some hard-core training.

That poem I wrote a few months after meeting him. I have put it here as chronologically; this is the time he entered my life.

Although I focused on the good and trusted, I must admit, my gut has never felt so uneasy. This training went on for a year or so and I learned a lot, but simultaneously things were strange and actually became very scary.

Another life lesson learned about the consequences of trusting too easily…

***

In the months that followed, life threw a variety of challenges my way. I wandered through dark corners and faced deep black holes. With the help of poetry, I found my resilience, bouncing back from tough times. It is not about being a victim, as I always choose to be a warrior; it is about turning vulnerability into strength…a journey we all share. The darkness is also to be explored with curiosity and to be experienced as it is part of the life experience helping us to learn, grow and transform.

23.   'Pain poem' 22.03.2022

Close your eyes, take a deep breath in.
Embrace the heartache… a familiar feeling.
I have been to this place before,
yet come out the other side its true.
So although I feel this pain strong and deep, I
 know I will get through.

This is just part of the adventure,
to trigger me to feel blue.
Feel my heart damaged and heavy,
a no motivation mood.

The pain that comes from a great love,
I let myself be open, vulnerable, yet more damageable too.

Although once again this life, my heart has truly broken,
A physical feeling inside my chest, the feeling that I am choking,
I decide not to be a victim by giving in to all the moping,
Nah- I would rather be floating!

My heart is full of gratitude for all that I have learned,

Lots of internal growth, love received, ceremonies with gifts earned.

The greater the pain mirrors the greatness of the love,

I feel full of appreciation for the connection of us,

two white doves.

Our adventures were clearly blessed from above,

44's everywhere, synchronicities and messages,

oh what love.

I learned some Spanish,

Made a drum,

Experienced squat life,

Had fun.

I learned to use my voice and to dance,

Have faith, take a chance.

I got to experience London life, become a master of the tube.

Learning new cultures, praying in a sweat lodge almost nude.

I met many interesting people- one gave me a tattoo!

So much deep internal learning and transformation too.

So I can see that even in my pain,

I can find the light.

The strength of my soul is unbreakable,

I don't even need to fight.

I just need to bear witness to the pain, as an observer...
The 'I', my soul, always there shining bright.
I am my own shiny armoured knight,
Saving myself from the depths of this dark night.

I surrender and let the pain encompass me.
I breathe through it and ground often with the tree.
I stay present in my senses, as a powerful me.

So many pain learnings recently!
A huge breakthrough was with the chilli!
A medicine woman put chillies in my eyes,
The pain was unspeakable, out of this world no surprise!
(I do not recommend)

The only way to cope with this excruciating pain,
Was to face it head on and transcend to another level of life's game.
A step within, to my soul, allowed me to be separate from it,
This was an intense journey, but too late to quit.

For one hour I sat in a meditation,
Truly experiencing what is pain.
Unable to open my eyes, move or speak to explain.
But I was able to transcend this,
Move consciousness to another lane.
Now what teachings from this I have claimed!

When the pain is too much, we can take a step in,
We can do this lying down, facing sky or ceiling.

Don't become the pain,
just observe it as an experience.
It is not you as it passes,
yet you are always present.

So far I have applied this technique when attending the dentist.
The injection didn't work,
so the pain of drilling my tooth was tremendous!
But I meditated and used the technique of going within,
I embraced the pain and released it, again and again.

This technique can be applied to emotional pain too,
So put this into practice is what I must do.

In addition, I trust life, there's always a reason,
Great pain brings great transformation,
then I'll be breezing,
Kingfisher, Blue Butterfly,
I'll open my wings and
Fly the universal flow,
new adventures beginning… AHO.

***

Trigger warning: Depiction of abortion To skip pg. 157)

24.   'Oh Baby' 26.06.2022

Oh sweet little baby,
You've come at a time when my head is crazy,
My vision feels blurred and my clarity is hazy,
Its been a tricky ride and I can't see what will save me.

Both options here bring me a feeling of sad,
Don't get me wrong,
having you in my life would make me feel glad,
But it's the guilt of not doing all the things I wish I had
And it's this guilt and self-loathing which could turn me mad

But to not meet you, really breaks my heart,
This so called 'treatment', I am dreading to start,
The guilt and shame of doing this may tear me apart,
I honestly feel like a right bumblaclart

Why is this happening, what is the reason?
I wish it had happened at a later season,
When I would truly be ready to raise my own son…
But instead, it is now, so what is the lesson?

This decision is crazy hard,
one that will be with me for life,
I just hope I make the right one,
so I am not tempted by the knife.

Currently my self-love and perception is at a serious low,
This honestly is such a big blow.
If I make the right decision or not,
how will I know?
I guess I just have to pick one,
then let go and flow.

One thing is true either way,
I love you with all my heart
Forever and a day.
My angel, my baby,
I hold your essence in my arms and sway,
I love you, I love you,
infinite times I will say.
AHO.

25.   'Hard times' 16.07.2022

Sometimes in life,
We feel we can no longer be here
Living this journey, this madness...
If you're feeling this way, open your ear.

Let's hold hands and journey through this together.
We can have our own and others backs
Through all stormy weather.
Also the grey days, sunny, windy too,
Through all life's experiences we can together get through.

First we must express,
our deepest thoughts and fears.
Embrace our own shadow, allow it to speak,
Only then our healing we can meet.

Express in words, to another
Or write it down, don't shudder.
Accept this part of you
and love it through and through.

When we only love our best self,
This is not true self-love.
We must accept our black raven
As well as our white dove.

The Ying Yang balance, around us, within us,
Once both accepted, we become whole, so try we must.

Once the darkness is expressed to yourself, face to face,
Then inner peace we can now co-create.
So first self-expression, that is a must.
Expression, acceptance, let go and then trust.
Trust you are held by loving hidden forces,
Now these are stronger than 10 billion forklifts!

Release the tension from your being.
Go back to square 1, SEE the world that you're seeing.

Breathe in,
Hold.
Breathe out.
Hold the intention of breathing in gold light
And breathing any heaviness out.

Do this now, as many times as feels right
Breathing deeply and mindfully clears our thinking, vision, sight.

It clears the chatter, the distractions, the blockages.
If we do this often there will be no stopping us.
Stay at this stage as long as you need,
Trust in divine flow and timing, you will succeed.

The letting go stage is a process for sure,
It keeps coming back,
Unwelcome thoughts at your door.

I feel them knocking now as I write these words,
But I trust that I will be free, divine timing, fly like a bird.

When we become focused on negative self-feeling,
It is our true happiness and peace we are stealing.
This thought alone can trigger more self-guilt, self-disgust,
The Bach flowers 'Pine' and 'Crab Apple' can help aid this if we
trust.
Again, breathe in, accept this feeling,
Then breathe it out, as a breath, surrender or shout.

Whatever your way, it's okay,
Just don't push it down.
Feel it fully, then release,
You will soon re-claim your inner kingdom crown.

26. 'Shadow' 09.09.2022

At times when our shadow comes forefront to play,
We can become our own barrier, a barrier hard to sway!
We may block ourselves off from opportunities,
Our perception of the world becomes dark and hazy.
At times like these the light and love can be harder to feel
and harder to see.
Know you are not alone;
this feeling has been felt by everybody.

Experienced in different ways of course,
no life paths are the same,
But we all have experienced a block from within,
during this life game.

This block can bring up different things for different people.
This block could create tears, self-loathing, hate.
It could create anxiety, anger, guilt or shyness around mates.

It can cause us to doubt ourselves, be misunderstood, hold
back.
When we hold back, our soul mission is hard to stay on track!

When we allow for fear of self-expression when we have a gut
feeling to act on,

We are cutting ourselves from flow and holding our spirit back
from,

Our destiny, opportunity, our chance to shine our light body.

I am learning that as our shadow and self-doubt rises,

That if we take a minute to meditate,

Our higher self can guide us.

That instead of recoiling in disapproval, shame, disgust,

It is giving genuine love to our shadow that do we must.

Self-love is not full when we only love our good parts,

hiding away our darker traits.

True self love is accepting all parts of self,

in a loving, gentle embrace.

We all have light and dark within us,

the ying yang balance of this game,

But to hold both in loving arms is to become whole again.

When experiencing fear, instead feel curious,

Remind self that there is no need to take life so serious.

Respect the shadow when it rises,

Listen, show compassion, then open to positive surprises!

Take a big breath, let go, trust the rest,

The flow of life will continue.

27. 'Curiosity' 29.09.2022

A learning for me,
Is the integration of the power of curiosity.

The curiosity which we were born with,
Young child exploring through play.
No fear, pure confidence,
Living fully present in each day.

Consciousness respawned onto this magnificent Earth,
Experiencing our senses,
A world vision is birthed!

Strong presence of curiosity,
Seeing, feeling, hearing, smelling
the flowers, sky, trees.
A lack of danger awareness which brings with it great
confidence,
You see children mad skateboarding, surfing, martial arts, flow
dance!

No fear of failure, which leads to success,
Persistence, self-belief, pure presence, mind at rest.

The children are our greatest teachers,
Connecting us to our inner child,
Unlocking the gifts we were given at birth…
As writing this I smiled.
Everything we need,
we were already given,
These gifts are never lost,
just sometimes they get hidden,
Deep within ourselves,
dimmed by the external world and our own shadow,
Causing us to forget our treasured gifts within-
mad one I know!

The process of remembrance is a journey,
may not happen in an instant-no,
For some it might- awesome!
But if not, don't fright,
Just trust in your journey being blessed by light.

Setbacks can happen and that is okay,
Try to focus on the positives and play or pray.

We must be mindful as adults,
The impact we have on children,
They are absorbent like sponges,
So we must be aware how we fill them.

Fill them with encouragement, belief, truth, respect, praise,

As it really does impact us, how we are raised.

If raised in challenging circumstances,

the parents are still learning,

Still living in a reality that their own parents served them.

Have compassion, send love, no resentment,

You can break the repeating pattern,

To positively influence the future generations,

Affecting society in turn.

New social norms and standards of respect will be learned.

So, stay connected with your perceptive lens of curiosity,

And a magical world of adventures, inspirations and awe

is what you will experience and see.

28.   'Perception' 01.10.2022

The world is the truth of our perception.
The energy we hold inside is mirrored in the external world-
reflection!

Our energy impacts the world we see,
It creates our own reality.
Heaven can be found on Earth,
If we can find peace within first.
This will enable a new world vision,
Beheld through our perspective lens,
To see each challenge, pain, lesson
As teachings helping us to transcend!

Closer to our higher self,
the oracle of our soul and past and future lives,
Connecting us closer to our remembrance-
beyond just THIS life!

Gathering more pieces of the puzzle,
towards the bigger picture,
Expanding our understanding and consciousness,
as explained in ancient scriptures.

An example of the power of perspective is when feeling instability,

No job, no house, no car, no loving family.

This perspective for some can trigger feelings of fear and insecurity.

Now the same circumstances can also be seen as being free!

Living in complete freedom, to ride the synchronistic flow,

following gut actions and feelings,

Trusting where to be and where to go.

This technique of shifting perspective can be applied to all situations we find ourselves in.

Most can be viewed in a positive light, even when challenging.

Remember the challenges are a gift, an opportunity,

To find our internal power,

Allowing us to blossom,

Blue star flower!

All of this practice is a lifetime's work.

But that is the primary work we came here to do...

To strengthen our whole being through,

Breathing through any fears, being curious of what might be,

if we take gut actions in confidence,

confident words and mind will follow suit- you'll see!

Go for it, see what happens, you hold the key!

The key to unlocking your full potential,

You radiant, glowing, pure spirit, with a body.

***

During the month of October 2022, I attended my first open mic night in a city and then a couple more open mic opportunities followed where I would share a poem (either 'Avatar' or 'Self-care toolkit') and worked on getting through the fears, breaking down the barriers and expressing myself. This felt so good! I felt my self-esteem increasing.

This was when my mum told me of a Qi Gong course happening in Thailand for one month with Tao master, Mantak Chia. I have not felt the desire to find another Qi Gong teacher following Jim. However, mum was keen, and I thought well there is nothing to lose. But to gain- a travel experience with my mum, opportunity for brain reset to climb out of my depression, and time and space to finally write this book and pull it all together. Once again, I thought f*ck it, savings are there to be spent! (I live for travel and experiences). So, we booked it, packed the same day and left the next and boom- off we went, leaving rainy windy England behind!

It was in Thailand where I began pulling this book together and some of the following entries were written whilst I was there.

29. 'Teachers' 09.11.2022

Teachers.

They are everywhere.

They are not only the guru's and experts in the world,

No,

They are everything and all you meet as your path unfurls!

When we keep our mind open to learn,

Every situation and conversation offers insights to be earned.

To expand our consciousness and broaden our perspective,

As everything and everyone together makes the collective.

Do not be closed to others,

Or make assumptions they have nothing to teach you…

Don't be blinded by a person's class, personality, status,

Or their differences to you.

Those pushed to the edges of society have lots of wisdom to offer-

See for yourself it's true!

You can learn so much from the homeless,

the imprisoned,

the disabled.

Don't be closed to interacting with people who are differently abled.

That just proves your judge mentality and shallow-ness.

Every person we meet on our path,

We meet for a reason with deeper purpose.

However, the teachings only come when we are open and curious,

Else we may block what learning the Great Spirit intended for us.

It's not just other humans we learn from,

No, it's nature and animals too,

One of my greatest teachers, My Dog Kody,

Has helped me through

Great depression, grief and sadness...

Walking with him in nature everyday- my heart was caressed,

I see that I am blessed!

He taught me to really SEE nature's beauty,

To stay present, be happy, be at one with the trees!

Nature herself teaches impermanence,

That change is inevitable,

So with it we must transform and dance!

It shows us the miracles of all and everything,

Just watch David Attenborough documentaries and you'll see what I mean!

Also remember, you are a teacher too.

Teaching many lessons to others on your path,

Many we may be unconscious to.

Never give in to the belief that you are just a follower,

Seeking all your answers externally,

or putting all eggs in the basket of one teacher.

A true guru or wisdom keeper will always guide you to look within,

Where universal secrets and wisdom are stored,

You hold the treasures of a King!

Allow others to guide you and absorb their teachings...

But remember your own experience is your real truth and understanding.

Respect others and all,

but worship none.

Value yourself and your own astral wisdom.

Trust divine timing, answers attained,

once learning is done.

When unsure close your eyes, breathe deep, feel in your heart,

Clear your mind, allowing space for insights to be won.

At times there may be none,
at others there will be some.
Be still until your gut feeling guides you to take an action.
Take your time, trust the process, no need to run.
Just be present, relax, soak in energy from the Sun.

You are your greatest teacher.
A journey of self-discovery and empowerment,
you began from day one.

***

Okay so the past two nights here in Thailand I have been having nightmares involving demons. This has been unpleasant and I have woken up sweating, hyperventilating or crying and then been unable to get back to sleep, feeling the fear emotion, feeling my kidneys aching and shrivelled, unable to relax. The kidneys are the organ which holds fear, so this makes complete and total sense. This negative experience has not happened in a long time (I have always been sensitive to feeling energies, but in recent years I have had mainly good experiences) so this has really caught me off guard. This morning when I woke up again, I felt drained, low mood, low energy and exhausted. My vibration low, attracting more low vibrational energies to me (law of attraction).. I engaged in some Qi Gong for my kidneys which has removed the physical kidney pain and helped get my energy moving again. At breakfast I realised that I am feeling resistance to going to sleep again tonight.

This triggered me to write a poem to express my feelings and find my inner strength and light again. Writing the below poem has helped me greatly, and right now I am feeling more in my power.

30.   'F*ck you Demons' 19.11.2022

F*ck you demons.
Leave me alone.
I did not invite you into my zone.
My zone is for compassion only,
I don't care if you are bored or you are lonely,
As you are messing with my head, my energy-
You are not being sacred, respectful or holy.

Show me love and compassion and I'll show you the same,
But mess with me once and you won't want to again.
As although you may view me as 'gentle' or 'innocent',
I have a fire inside and quick temper when I am faced with
maleficence
(This attribute of me is due to my Mars in Leo,
The aggression of a lion- uh oh for you I know!)

That's right I am a light warrior,
And yes, you are right to let this worry ya,
Because light destroys all darkness and is much stronger,
When a light is turned on at night, the darkness is no longer.

I refuse to give into fear and let you feed off these emotions.

No, I will stay grounded with Mother Earth and breathe my gold light energy in motion.

I refuse to drink your evil, control, manipulation potion.

I will shine brighter with FEROCIOUS love and devotion.

Just because I'm love and light does not mean I am a "pussy",

As love and light takes more strength- a peaceful feisty warrior,

So don't even try to fight me.

Although, "pussy", would actually be a complement,

As the power of the womb, the yoni-verse can be equally dominant.

Pussy power all the way!

Creative centre- making magic and protection to keep the darkness away.

Anyway, I am digressing, now back to the point of this poem...
F*ck you demons!

Now with all the warnings above being said,

know that if you show me compassion,

I will reflect this.

I hold no judgements and will see the love in you,

if and when you are ready to accept it.

31.'Death' 19.11.2022

Death is a mad one.

It can be a sad one.

For others it's a glad one.

But to it many are just numb.

It's often an unspoken topic.

When brought up in conversation, many want to change it quick!

It can be like the large dark elephant in the room,

And without spiritual beliefs, it really is all doom and gloom.

To believe that when your physical body dies, that is the total end...

To think that's it, POOF, disappeared into darkness,

is a western mind set trend.

What a depressing thought,

giving the impression that this life is random and has no real purpose...

This can leave the subconscious feeling that we as individuals are worthless.

Instead, why not believe that when our bodies die it's NOT the end...

Instead, our soul, our spirit, the 'I', just transforms and
transcends.

Goes to another level, another room of existence if you like.

There are rumours and teachings that this next place

can actually be more bright.

What if when we die, our journey is actually just beginning?

That this life times aim

was just to put our spirit through training.

Preparing us for new adventures, experiences and learning.

So do be mindful your impact in this life- karmas real

so doing bad things is concerning.

Remember with our actions, there are always consequences,

Which can for sure stay with us across the different dimensions.

So don't get distracted by instant gratification-

power, money, selfish greed.

These things don't account to good karma if used negatively

to make only yourself 'succeed'.

Don't neglect your spirituality,

Remove the blinkers so the value of this you can see.

Strengthen your spirit and compassion to broaden

your next level opportunities.

It is also said that when we pass over to the other side,

We release all pain and dense emotions, leaving suffering behind.

We are also able to re-connect with loved ones,

for whom many tears we have cried,

Because above all and everything,

Remember,

Great Spirit is kind.

***

The empowerment of the F*ck you Demon's poem worked! I have not had nightmares since! I asked for extra protection and guidance and then fully trusted that I have this.

32.　　　'Trust' 20.11.2022

Having trust is everything.
It is crucially important.
It can keep us protected and safe.
It can manifest us abundance.

During times of worry,
Uncertainty, stress or fear,
We must trust we are supported by God, good spirits,
loved ones and angels, knowing they are near.
Holding us, protecting us,
Guiding us and directing us.

Ask out loud for help and then relax
and trust you are receiving.
The power of this is unstoppable,
when we are fully believing.
As our intent, belief and trust creates our reality-
The truth we are perceiving.

Don't accept others disbelief of this as fact,
for them it may not be truth,
But that's because they are not yet practicing and achieving.

The more you believe,

The more life support you will receive.

Believe you are worthy of being supported,

Know that you are held in love- don't let your mind distort this.

Trust you are powerful, radiant and strong.

Trust in yourself and spirit and you won't be wrong.

Trust in the pull and guidance of your heart song,

Trust in your ability to ask for help, don't bite your tongue.

Trust that all the pain experiences,

are for your learning and greater good.

Trust that if not now, then later

the peaks and troughs will be understood.

Trust that everything passes,

especially the depressive no motivation moods.

Trust that the sun will rise each day,

trust in the magic of the woods.

Trust you will take correct action, perfect timing,

don't be held to 'should's or could's'.

Trust in the power of your energy,

trust in the good intention you put in your food.

Trust in yourself, you know what to do,

Know that no one else has ever 'walked in your shoes'.

So, to summarise TRUST TRUST TRUST,
there is nothing to lose.
Raising your energy to the trust vibration,
will attract positive situations to you.

Open your heart to receive love and support,
And then express your gratitude.

***

In Thailand I met an amazing person and traveller called Ben. It was for sure part of the universe's bigger plan for us to meet, as he caught my attention in a second-hand bookstore and then happened to be in the next shop I went into too! We began talking and wow his life story he shared with me is incredible and shocking.

Ben has experienced true terror- living through wars his whole life. What he shared with me touched me greatly and some of it shocked me too.

Ben inspired me so much as despite all the challenges he has faced- he is so smiley, open, sociable and ready to connect with others. A true inspiration and figure of strength…. I mean the strength of his spirit is unbreakable. He teaches me that no matter what we go through and experience, always try to keep our hearts loving and have a smile available to others.

Like the lotus flower which can grow through murky muddy waters and still blossom so beautifully. The below poem is based on some of Ben's life experience he shared with me.

Much love Ben.

33.   'Inspired' 02.12.2022

I am super inspired…
Inspired by the power and strength of love-
This is something to be truly admired.

Despite the physical and mental raging war and danger all around,
Even in the darkest nights, the strength of love can be found.

In the small acts of kindness, of utmost simplicity,
Yet in the circumstances takes courage to remain in connectivity.
In these moments we experience or witness souls' electricity.

The high vibration of energy,
contrasting with the surrounding dense frequency.
A striking contrast so its impact felt immensely.

Imagine living in a place where the norm is PTSD…
The baseline- so your suffering is not heard or seen.
This is the anxiety standard of living.
Lack of support and help, as all are suffering.
Told to get on with it and not make a scene…

Only bedtime- alone- is space for crying.

No one feels like dancing or singing,

As people are only just coping.

This is happening in many places around the world,

how very distressing.

Imagine being told as a child on the bus,

To be aware it could any second blow up!

Told to watch for any bags unattended, left behind,

Watch for men in big jackets on hot days- suicide on their mind.

Living in fear for all you go near,

Everyday survival completely unclear.

Imagine missiles raining all around you as a teen,

You feel this is it,

your last moment is coming,

You jump out your car and run behind a rock,

weed ready to be lit

But then you realise you have no lighter - Ah Sh*t!

Ready to run to your car to retrieve your flame,

So you can be high and find some relief during your last
moments in this life game.

Then over the rock jumps a panicked man,

You tell him to breathe and calm himself if he can.

You ask him for a light, giving him a distraction,

And the smoking of the spliff is then sparked into action.

You enjoy this smoke but then have an intuition to move,

Jump in the car, drive through the bombs,

your favourite pub is the place to die you choose.

You order a pint and sit down with the lads together,

Heart racing but connected in these last moments,

ready to leave this current life forever.

This powerful love in the darkness...

to find we must endeavour.

Somehow you made it through the night, and continue living,

A gift but many scars were given.

This is not the only time you've held fear for your life

and been driven,

Into flight, fight and survival mode,

making life changing decisions.

Feeling fear, anger, sadness or revenge,

but these expressions are invisibly forbidden.

During your time of forced service,

you have injuries that are critical,

Impacted by bombs and exploding shrapnel,

Dragged into a family home by your comrades,

Your main concern not your life,

but the children's eyes you'd rather save.

Save from this gruesome image of fear, blood and war,

Leaving children worried about what's next through their door.

In this moment the 'opponent countries' mother of this house
(the 'enemy') is collecting all her medicines,

Dropping them around you for the medics' attention.

Freezing cold and she wraps you in a blanket,

love in her eyes as for you she tries to comfort.

This act of love and selflessness is the most inspiring,

Especially when the world around appears to be collapsing.

Let us all take this as a powerful teaching,

To share acts of kindness to all that we meet,

Everyone has experienced inner or outer war and terror,

or both,

But to find our strength to radiate love in these times,

can be our sacred oath.

34.   'Near death experience' 03.12.2022

So this week I had a near death experience,

Impending doom and helplessness- I felt so serious!

My small intestine was super blocked,

A blockage I didn't know how to unlock.

I felt super full and super-hot,

A temperature, lots of pain, damn you psyllium husk!

Someone gave me this and I had too much followed by a hot dehydrated day at some hot springs... this supplement expands inside the body, and I had not had enough fluid to flush it through...learning I should always research supplements before taking them!

I stopped eating for 3 days,

Did lots of Qi Gong,

Saw a healer for an organ massage called chi Nei Tsang ('Chinny sung')

My problem was that I gave into fear,

I allowed panic and darkness near.

I lost my power and I became weaker,

Accepting my poor state- future looking bleaker.

My black and white mind,

Swinging from trust and surrender

To preparing for death, thinking I won't survive.

An intense imagination,

Capable of miracle or horror story creation,

I can believe both extreme ends of the spectrum.

I mean I once believed on Easter day that Jim would appear-
resurrection

All day I waited in the woods feeling joyous suspension...

Young teen me also believed I would be murdered in the field
every day on the way to school-,

much fear and apprehension.

This stemmed from watching a film called 'The lovely bones'
and making a connection.

I believe in magic and I believe in ghosts,

I believe in unicorns and I believe in cursed toads.

I believe anything is possible,

My minds imagination can run away- unstoppable.

This can be a blessing, or this can cause big trouble,

It can literally create or burst my protective light bubble.

So you see this blocked digestive situation

Had my mind scattered, unsure of my next step or destination.

It made me feel helplessness and frustration,

Solution and answers? I knew none!

Everything conflicted in my head,

Realistic ideas that I will soon be dead.

I had to change the thought patterns...

I decided to trust in the universe and allow my spirit to be led.

In the nights leading up to this moment,

Whilst in bed I felt surrounded by dark energies- super potent!

But once I decided to keep my faith,

That the universe holds me, I will be okay.

To call on God, my angels and guides and trust they are there,

I relaxed more and more as I felt held and for cared.

My mum was the best and took action to stop my mind from spinning,

She knows me well, so knew if I continued in my panic there would be no winning.

The doctor at the hospital was so kind and reassuring,

The days that followed I had to keep faith and not to fear give in.

When my mind relaxed, my body did too,

When I accepted love and healing

From all those around me, I was receiving.

My body was mending, I was no longer grieving.

My spirit strength was tested, but finally I'm rested.

My body is recovering, I feel blessed and

From this experience I take away many lessons...

My body is a temple so food I must feed it with the best ones,

Filling all that enters my body with gratitude and good intentions.

Also, I have learned that we got to have faith, faith,

trust and faith,

That we are held and supported whist asleep and awake.

We are so loved- when we love and trust our self,

The universe responds accordingly- see for yourself!

Affirm- I am protected, strong, cared for and held,

I know and trust that I deserve this – surplus!

Speak prayers aloud as they are then heard-

Our Loving Magic Spells.

***

Shortly after this intense health experience, we left Tao Gardens after one month of learning and practicing 'Inner alchemy Qi Gong' and connecting with our 'family' of friends with who had come from all over the world. A very blessed experience. We travelled to Bangkok and from there, Mum went back to England and I went south to Koh Phanang Island for a 2-week solo travel.

35.   'Go with your flow' 05.12.2022

Today the waterfall empowered me,
To remember the power in surrendering to flow,
Releasing all tension held subconsciously,
Teaching me to truly let it all go.

When I woke up this morning I felt in a dark rut,
Feeling imbalanced in my mind and in my gut,
Did my routine but then got back to bed and my eyes I re-shut.
I lay in gratitude for the jungle hut
And for all experiences and gifts of life, but...
Somehow, I could not shake this depressiveness,
I could not access that other feeling of pure bliss and
righteousness.

I did my Qi Gong flow,
had a coconut on the beach,
did some writing,
but my creativity hard to reach.

Needed to do something different, clear my head,
So to the waterfalls I was led,

A red and black dragonfly inspiring this journey,
each step of the way appearing to me.

Walked many steep roads- only walker in sight!
Explored 3 waterfalls to the right.
Stood on a big rock, rain began to shower,
I stood in it and started singing- regaining my power.
'Let it be' I sang on repeat,
One of my favourites- A tough one to beat,
Just those 3 words
Allowed my spirit and the divine to again meet.

I was reminded to trust in the universe again and again,
It has been proven a million times,
no need to forget this and go insane.
Must remember it's not always clear in the moment,
And often to get the gift we must first go through the hurt.

But when in this process,
Don't allow absolute faith to digress,
Away from the path of trust,
which when we're on, brings less stress.

I followed my free-flowing intuition and the black and red dragonfly,
Up to the 'hide on high' cliff top bar- getting there was a trek mind!

I was the only customer all afternoon,
So, I made friends with the man who runs it,
and lives there too.

He was so kind,
he gave me cooked potatoes to dip into sugar,
He chilled with me
and gave me coconut water,
He cooked me fresh omelette and rice,
So delicious I ate it twice!

He then gave me a snickers bar,
when I mentioned something sweet,
Ah I'm so grateful the universe guided me to this meet.

The food was fresh and healthy, good for my tummy-
Except for the snickers bar, but it was so yummy!
He has given me lots of useful info,
all about the island that I would not have known,
he has offered to take me to a night market this evening on his
motorbike,
he's going there anyway, so I guess I might!

Doors have opened after I prayed that they would,
Now I must flow in my rivers flow,
Take risks, trust, surrender, let go.

***

So, the Solo travel in Thailand was so good! I made friends with many Thai locals, lived in a hut in the jungle, went to Muay Thai boxing, learned Thai cooking, went waterfall hopping, made new friends and had spontaneous adventures and had some crazy off-road motor bike experiences! It was an amazing experience which blossomed from having trust, surrendering and letting go. Not planning ahead and just being super present and open to all experiences that presented themselves to me. A great lesson and putting into practice my current learning of trust. Trusting others, trusting the universe and trusting that I am always held, and my life is unfolding for the highest good of all.

When we can live in a more consistent state of this, our energy raises frequency and vibration, and we are carried with the flow of life and not resisting this flow and stagnating.

However, an important note is to only 'go with the flow' when in a state of peace and trust. It is a different experience to go with the flow when in a state of fear, anxiety or anger, as that will be the flow that we are attracting. When in that state, we must first put in the work to change our internal state and then once we have achieved our internal balance and high vibration internally, that is when we can relax to go with the flow as we have already created our energy field of high vibration and trust, which will tune us in to receive a life of that frequency. Always tend to your safety.

This is part of our lifetimes practice. The more often we attend to feeling inner peace, the less is needed to be done to maintain it.

***

This year I went to a tantric communication workshop at a summer festival, and it was insightful. I have been putting into practice what I learned; about really allowing space for another to talk and not feeling the need to speak in order for them to know I am listening. This can take the expression of the person away from the message they are trying to express.

I wrote the next poem here in Thailand thinking about that, as it was interesting engaging with other travellers and also observing group conversations. When people allow the person to express all of what they want, the energy of expression and attention will move freely and flow between members of the group, who have an insight to share in that moment which all can learn from.

When everyone is trying to express at once and therefore interrupts others, the whole conversation is jagged and stilted and there becomes a power struggle of energy and no one's full message is expressed. We must all learn to listen attentively to others and hold space for their expressions. If we all do this, everyone will feel heard, understood and connected. When we do this for others they will mirror this back to us, so try this with those around you. Observe how once they are fully expressed, not only will you learn more, but you will be truly respecting and connecting with that person, who is then able to also hold space for you.

36.   'Listen Properly: Tantric Communication' 07.12.2022

When talking with others be sure to listen properly,
Tune into what they are saying,
Don't be engrossed in thoughts of 'me'.
Tantric communication is another word for it
To allow space for another to have their spotlight lit
To not interrupt their expression is a true gift.

When we butt in with comments or other ideas,
We take the person off their train of thought,
Making it hard for them to express their message clear.

Allowing the other to talk,
allows their wisdom and teachings to come through,
Benefitting all present and allowing magic to brew.

How good it feels when someone listens to us
with open ears and patience,
Then an equal opportunity for each to share
the stage is awakened.

Complete respect and connection is achieved,

No rush to get words out before interrupted,

so our mind is at ease.

More difficult this can be in groups,

As there can be more conversation loops.

All present have to be aware how to interact like this,

That's why in ceremonies they may use a talking stick,

Which gives space for that person to express what they wish

Which may be long, or may be quick.

So next time you engage in conversation,

check in that you are allowing silence and space

for what the other is saying.

You may even get answers to what you have been for praying.

So, listen properly and it's the standard you're changing,

You will notice people will hold space for you the same and,

Wisdom will be shared.

Each and every day is our training.

I returned from Thailand, trip of a lifetime, so much gratitude! I spent Christmas at home which was lovely spending time with family and friends and KODY (I missed him so much and was sending him love and connection in meditation daily!

***

January 2023: Life has been a bit wild again.

I thought I was close to finishing this book, but then I hit a bout of writer's block. Part of it stemmed from not feeling good. To be honest with you, I felt like I was on the verge of a mental breakdown triggered by challenging life circumstances and environment once I returned from my trip. I was also very unsure about my next move regarding work and where to live. It also dawned on me that I was not prioritising my self-care practices enough. While I was doing some each day, it was not sufficient given the intense emotions I was experiencing.

So, I decided to step up my game. I began meditating every morning and night, setting intentions for the day. I started incorporating a workout into my morning routine and engaged in more Qi Gong. I also reached out to my angels and guides for support. Long, leisurely walks in nature with Kody. I allowed myself to just be and made self-care my top priority, as it always should be. I have come to understand that the only way I can truly be of service to others and the world is by first taking care of myself. After all, I am a part of this world, and the state of this part has the most significant impact on the surrounding parts. It is how the interconnectedness works.

I have known all this before and have lived it. It is fascinating how life is a constant evolution and recalibration of ourselves, reminding us of what we already know when we have been too immersed in the intricacies of the matrix. We can heal and then experience events which require more healing to be done. Healing is a non-stop conscious effort and throughout life we will for sure go through numerous trials and tribulations, teaching us increased strength, resilience, and ways of being.

When we zoom out and remind ourselves of the bigger picture of the life we are living, it becomes evident that each of us is on our unique and fascinating journey, crafting our own story. We could all write a book about our experiences and inspire others. Many parts of our stories would be relatable, fostering a sense of connection and alleviating feelings of loneliness. We are each connected through our individual experiences, which, at their core, offer feelings which are the same. We are never alone.

A crucial factor affecting my mental state during this time was the delay in my moon cycle. My last cycle was 52 days long! It was perplexing because there was no chance I could be pregnant, so where was my period?

I figured it out. During my time in Thailand and experiencing my 'near-death experience,' my body underwent significant stress. According to my 'Flo' tracking app, it predicted that my ovulation day for my last cycle coincided with the day I went to the hospital in Thailand.

Stress, particularly around this time of the cycle, can hinder the release of the egg. I believe this is what happened to me. So, I had a buildup of PMS hormones in my body waiting to be released, but my period did not arrive for three more weeks! Engaging in my daily self-care practices massively helped my body relax. No wonder I felt so mentally unstable; hormones play a significant role in our well-being and balance. I even entertained the thought of a phantom pregnancy from one of my encounters with spirits in Thailand (not a pleasant one). When my period finally arrived, I felt an overwhelming sense of gratitude and emotional release—it was beautiful. I feel so much better now.

Our menstrual cycles are sacred and deserve respect instead of closed-minded disdain. They profoundly affect all women, offering valuable insights into ourselves, when we are aligned with our cycles (not taking contraception, which dysregulates our whole system).

It is during our time of bleeding that our intuition peaks. Where we bleed in accordance with the moons cycle is also very insightful. Refer to the appendix at the end for more information about red, white, pink and purple moon cycles.

***

Super inspiring just now. I got home from Kung Fu and took Kody out for a walk in the snow and the stars and went to the family Oak tree. This is such a legendary tree and has always been a key point for our family and its history. My Grandad William was especially connected with this tree; he passed over 6 years ago, and we often go there to connect with him and feel his wisdom, strength and love come through. Legend.

Right now, I am in a 'hurricane moment' of external life happenings. Yet I feel completely peaceful inside. I feel unmovable. Unshakable. Pure love and peace. Thank you. When I was with the Oak, we were one, and the next poem came to my mind.

37.　　　'Oak in a hurricane' 18.01.2023

Here I stand under the branches of the Oak tree,
Gazing up to the stars, many constellations I can see…
Here I am a connector between the Earth and Sky…
yep that's me,
as with everything else in this beautiful reality,
All the people, animals, vegetation and trees
This is so magical like an imagined fantasy,
Each of us connectors, flowing channels of energy,
What we choose to add to this energy is our will power,
our thoughts and actions- real synergy.

We must learn that what we feed it
impacts the world we perceive.
Like the somewhat twisted story of Adam and Eve.
If we feed it with 'sin' like intentionally causing pain and crying,
Not speaking our truth,
or worse, harmful lying,
Only negative energy we are cultivating
and negative experiences towards us this will bring.

Instead, we feed the energy with gratitude and love,

Being centred and present, trusting,

guided by the stars above,

And the Earth below,

guiding our footsteps as we go.

Harmonising our thoughts, words and actions,

Negativity melts away like warm snow.

They say the outer reality mirrors our internal,

This is true as our thoughts and feelings attract the same frequency of energy.

We become a magnet for where the focus of our thoughts lead.

If we focus on things that were sad or when we have been done wrong,

we blind our vision from seeing all of life's beauty and sweet songs.

Embrace any pain, accept and move on,

As holding onto this hurts yourself, but also everyone.

Choose to breathe through it,

zoom out and see the bigger picture.

Be the bigger person, be your higher self,

add love and courage to the mixture.

By living this way,

processing and transforming when we forgive,

A much free-er happier life we get to live.

Don't swallow the scorpion that stung you,

Instead, understand others perspectives and why they did what they did.

Once we are able to maintain the inner peace inside,

The hurricane will calm itself on the outside.

This balanced, centred feeling, the strong Oak does know.

When we stay solid in love at our centre,

even the strongest winds cannot stub our toe,

Life includes chaos and pain as we all know.

So always remember, you can be the

Peace within a Hurricane-

The strong Oak shows us so.

***

So, yeah, we are connectors between everything, Earth and Sky energy balanced and flowing within us. We are nurtured by and grounded to the Earth, uplifted to the sky. And we can influence that energy to expand it in love or contract it, depending on how we choose to feed it. When we manage to find balance, we become stable and protected within ourselves, by ourselves. We become our own Oak. Then, no matter what life throws at us, we cannot be broken or destroyed. We are powerful when we live in love.

Do not worry if you do not yet know this feeling; it is something we are all working towards, a lifetime's work, always requiring present intention.

Reflecting on my life, it has often been defined as 'intense' by others, and I feel it that way too. I experience extreme highs and then extreme lows. But then I realised something: the external reality we experience is a reflection of our internal reality. And indeed, my internal world can be intense. However, this is just who I am—the 'Autistic' black and white brain—it is simply how I am designed. I can still find peace within the intensity, but it may explain why I seem to experience such intense life events.

My friend Robyn, whom I met in Thailand, once told me that she feels my life is full of intensity so that I can experience things. These experiences are what inspire my writing, serving as a way for me to express what I am living. She suggested that this is part of my soul mission—by living these experiences and sharing my ways of coping and overcoming challenges, I may support others who are experiencing something similar or relatable. It is a way to connect us all over the world through our shared experiences.

Drop identities, cultures, religions, prejudices, and embrace that we are one race, the human race. We each walk unique life paths with different sets of challenges, missions, and focuses. We just have to find the thing that lifts us. Our passions. Our way of opening and lifting our hearts and our energy. That feeling is how we know that we are on the right path. It is the feeling that is important, less so is the way in which we get there.

A lesson I learned though this recent mental set back was about discipline with my daily practices. Self-care and re-centring is so important for us to maintain our equilibrium and wellbeing- especially if you have an intense mind same as me! Emotional regulation can be harder when the mind is intense, so it is so helpful to engage in things which maintain that balance.

Discipline with self is key.

38.   'Discipline' 22.01.2023

Discipline, discipline, discipline.

Self-discipline, the biggest action of self-love.

This is how in this life we will win.

When mastering self-discipline,

Put laziness in the bin.

Time for a motivation mind set, put yourself in.

It's really worth getting out of bed in the morning and trying

To start the day

with self-care for you,

in whichever way.

This could be stretching, meditation,

yoga, a cup of tea.

It could be a workout, walk in nature,

writing a gratitude diary.

Setting your intention of the day,

paving out the way,

For a day full of magic and contentment,

in joy and love you will sway.

Asking God, guides and angels for help and guidance,

you just have to say.

Work hard but don't forget to play,

Always stay present, as you are always in today.

Gratitude. I have found this to be the simplest and most effective way to shift my reality into positivity and contentment. In 2017 I read a book called 'The Secret' by Rhonda Bryne. This is one of those books which changed my life greatly, for the better. For those who are not familiar with this book, in a nutshell it discusses and explores the power of gratitude. It explains how when we feel true gratitude, which is accompanied by that warm, uplifted, open feeling in the heart. This raises our energetic frequency to this vibration and, as explained by the law of attraction, attracts more situations in our external world to align with us, as they are the same frequency. Think of tuning into a radio station and then being able to access those songs.

When I read 'The Secret' I began writing a gratitude diary EVERYDAY - this helps to affirm our thoughts and feelings of gratitude. What this does is shift our perspective and focus, to focus on all the good things, not the bad. In every situation there is always a good and bad way to perceive it, we can focus on the light or the dark; both are always present as one cannot exist without the other. However, we can sometimes get stuck in a negativity thought pattern cycle and become overly focused on the negative, which results in us feeling bad and can lead us to be stuck in a dark hole. I realised in that engaging in gratitude practices is a simple and very effective version of CBT (Cognitive behavioural therapy).

I was referred to CBT to help my mental health when I was 17, but it was not for me. I found the sessions I went to, to be very focused on the negative thoughts and where they came from, which can be beneficial to address the root cause (e.g. inner child work), but is not good to dwell extensively on this emotion from history as that makes us not focus on the present, when often the present moment is pleasant. I found the gratitude practice much simpler and more positive as I like to focus on the positive thoughts as they make me feel good and raise my energy frequency vibration. Where attention goes, energy flows.

I have continued to engage in gratitude practice regularly although I have not been so consistent with my gratitude diary recently (stopped doing it daily).

I am ready to build it into my daily routine again. I enjoy tuning into my gratitude before I get out of bed and before I go to sleep, reflecting on the day and all of its gifts and blessings, big and small.

Thank you, thank you, thank you.

39.   'Gratitude' 26.01.2023

The most life enhancing thing we can do,

Is to live in a state of pure gratitude.

It is the most magical attitude,

And a beautiful living it leads to.

For when we live in gratitude and stay present to the gift that is this life,

We invite more positive experiences in and take them in our stride.

Let us tune in and really receive what we are receiving,

Each moment is a miracle, we best be believing.

Life can change in an instant,

can't take anything for granted,

Appreciate each moment,

To life be enchanted.

Grateful for our eyes with which we can see,

Grateful for our spirits temple which is our beautiful body.

Grateful for the Earth, all the trees and species,

Grateful for the food from which we can grow from the seeds.

Grateful for the Sky, the warmth, light and wonder,
Grateful for our unique minds and for new ideas we can ponder.

Grateful for the water to drink,
the food to eat,
being able wash our hands at a sink.

Grateful for the stranger's smile,
the child's laugh,
elders with so much wisdom on file

Grateful for those we love and our own self and inner child,
Grateful to ourselves for always being there and showing up,
no day off- pretty wild!

Grateful to all ancestors, angels and guides,
Grateful to the spirit animals always by our side.
Grateful for the greatness and depth of this creation,
Grateful for the continual wonder of the totality of everything,
Grateful for this life and its Creator.

Truly, what a blessing.

And oh, what Gratitude we can have towards The Earth and Sky, which hold and contain us, providing us with everything we could ever need… and we are part of them.

40.   'Mother Earth' 13.11.2022

Mother Earth,
I thank you.
I appreciate you.
I love you.

Thank you for all you provide me with,
A beautiful place I can call home,
All the beauty and inspiration,
The nourishing food- best chef known!

Thank you for the mountains, rivers, jungles, deserts, forests.
Thank you for the sea, lakes, soil, flowers,
you really are the best!

Thank you for the animals and all the unique,
intelligent creatures,
Each with their own special powers,
even blowing minds of science teachers!
Thank you for the crystals and minerals,
Nature's wisdom bearers.
Thank you for holding all those lived before us,
all our beloved ancestors!

Thank you for being one home, one plane,

You created no borders.

You are so balanced and intricate,

You made zero errors.

Thank you for all the plant teachers and master medicines,

When engaging with them in ceremony and intention,

Our soul they help heal and transcend!

Beautiful gifts which allow us to see again,

The veil is lifted, magic is understood as real again,

Allowing us to be whole and compassionate,

beautiful men and beautiful women.

Mother I appreciate all you are and all you do.

I appreciate you holding me in unconditional love,

Helping me to view,

The world through a positive lens again,

Especially when I'm feeling blue.

I never have to wait for your attention or line up and que.

You are there, always present, open arms to help me through.

When I feel suffering, pain or despair,

I am brought to the Earth, lying on my back,

drained of care.

I realise now why I instinctively do this,

It's because you are always there!

To hold me, to ground me,

To transmute the negative feelings I can no longer bare.

You take away the pain and give me back gold light,

Making me an energetic millionaire!

I am worthy of love and respect,

Especially from myself,

You made me aware.

There is no other love that can compare,

You are always giving and always fair.

Now it is our turn, as humanity, to help you repair.

I love you; I love you,

I'll shout it from the mountain top to declare!

I want to support you and help you,

So with others the current system we must tear,

To change our lifestyle and way of living we must dare.

Building self-sustaining communities is the correct path,

but not an easy affair!

I don't have all the answers or the ultimate solution,

I just have a strong spirit,

and want to be part of the team to get this done.

Time to let go of comforts, excess, consumerism, greed.

We must go back to basic living if we are to succeed.

Balanced Flame

I love you mother,
Along with so many others.

Thank you for always holding us in love,
Me and all my sisters and brothers.

41.'Father Sky' 14.11.2022

Father Sky,
I Thank you.
I Appreciate you.
I Love you.

Thank you for watching over Mother Earth and all of us.
Thank you for protecting us and literally holding this world
together,
A real plus!

Thank you for the gifts your rain brings,
Washing away our pain and purifying our being.
The rain which allows Mother Earth to grow and flourish,
Helping food to grow so our bodies we can nourish.

Thank you for the Sun, providing us with warmth,
Light and energy,
Lighting up this world, giving life
and allowing us to see!

Thank you for the wind, cleansing away all the heaviness,
Leaving a feeling of refreshment, clarity and newness.

Thank you for the white fluffy clouds,

So soft and squishy like candy floss.

I enjoy watching them,

My imagination creating stories,

Insightful messages received at no cost!

Thank you for the wondrous sunrises and sunsets,

A magnificent daily reminder of one of the creator's artistic outlets.

You remind us of your vastness when in the sky we see the seemingly 'small' jumbo jets.

Thank you for the lightning and the thunder,

Their strength and power have me in wonder!

They shake things up, clean the stagnant energy out,

The intense electric of the lightning,

The loud thunder shout.

Thank you for the oxygen you provide in the air,

Allowing us to breathe and therefore live,

So this life experience we can share.

Thank you for the magic of the rainbows,

Chakra colours in the sky refracted.

Lead me to find my internal pot of gold,

Just witnessing a rainbow, my spirit is fulfilled and attracted!

Thank you for the Moon, each month working its magic,

Guiding our personal cycles

and helping us develop healthy habits.

Thank you for the stars, sparkle sparkle in the night sky,

Thank you for all the shooting ones,

Providing wishes to those who see them with their eye.

Thank you for the star signs which impact our destiny,

Thank you for all the planets, all too impacting us intensely!

I appreciate your expansiveness.

My mind is blown knowing that when I look up

there is no end or perimeter I can express!

So when I look up, this space before my eyes could be infinite!

A subtle reminder that our abilities and dreams also have no
limit, so remain passionate.

I can stare at the sky for hours,

it brings me so much awe, peace and joy.

When feeling overwhelmed, sad or stressed, do this technique
so our emotions don't destroy,

Our spirit, our light...

Nah-Look to the Sky, zoom out and enjoy.

Enjoy the possibilities of this existence.

Turning to face the Sky whenever needing inspiration or guidance.

As they say reach for the stars, don't worry about the distance.

Ask the Sky to help expand your consciousness,

self-belief and confidence.

I love you Father Sky,

You give me a natural high.

You clear my tears when in my eyes I cry,

Your unconditional love soothes me, takes away my sigh.

Thank you for holding me, making me feel so alive.

I will appreciate you always,

Every day until I die.

***

I have not written in a while... I was invited to London and began working as an OT through the NHS supporting children in the community. It has been a busy, interesting and challenging time. I have not enjoyed the city life- so dirty and busy and stress energy in the air. I have not been sleeping well and due to living arrangements (and motivation), not eating well either. I have missed Kody a lot and I have felt very alone and cut off from family and nature. My self-care slacked and therefore my mental health and scarily my physical health.

I am the most ill I have ever been. The pain is focalised in my womb and comes in random bouts of stabbing pain which drops me to the floor screaming in pain (and I am a quiet person). I have been so swollen and had so much pain I have ended up in A and E twice (given lots of gas and air). Both times doctors told me there was nothing wrong with me and it is all in my head.

My own research and interactions with other women were indicating signs of endometriosis. This is a scary disease and I have seen friends of mine severely impacted by this, impacting daily life and spreading to other organs. They too were told by the Doctors that there was nothing wrong, yet have gone on to have surgery to remove parts of their internal organs.

I left London and came home to heal. I knew my lifestyle of poor sleep and diet and being away from Kody was impacting me negatively, so this was the first step. I got worse for a while before I got better... I lost so much weight as anything I would eat caused me severe pain as I was so inflamed. It was scary. The doctors said they wanted to test me for cervical cancer. When I rang up for the results the receptionist told me that there was a result my doctor needed to discuss with me. My mind at that time was such a whirlwind of panic and fear I automatically thought I had cancer. I had to wait until the Monday to speak with the doctor, so 2 and a half days believing I had cancer and was dying. My overreactive mind. Turned out, this was not the news she was to tell me, it was a lot more minor. Thankful.

221

My sister told me to try having protein shakes, as I was losing muscle and had no energy (still majorly inflamed womb though). This helped and I was able to stomach it and gradually my energy came back as I was able to provide my body with some fuel. Once my energy came back, I had more energy to sort my mind.

My mind had become a toxic place, and I knew I needed to heal this first before I could heal my body, as the two are so intrinsically connected. I began with positive affirmations. I wrote five A4 pages of them after reading 'You can heal your life'.(!) I wrote about my body being perfectly healthy well and balanced, my thoughts being positive and kind, feeling safe and supported at all times etc. Every morning, I would sit in front of the mirror and read these out loud, looking into my own eyes.

I also began making the anti-inflammation green juice daily that the London Uber driver told me about (mentioned at beginning of the book near self-care toolkit poem). This Uber driver was a gift from God. I made this drink every day and added dandelions and plantain leaves from the fields I foraged with Kody.

Gradually I was getting better and was able to eat again. I went back to Ayurvedic (Indian healing through food) meals (lots of mung bean soup) and practices as they were easiest for me to digest.

I began mediation and getting back into my Qi Gong practice. The pain was reducing. I believed in the power of my mind and visualised myself happy and well every day.

I had to begin work again and just did part time hours with ASD children OT assessments. Although I did not feel fit for work, I needed the money, as in London I had been scammed by a fraudulent agency who stole half of my money owed for the full five months and disappeared as though he had never existed. This was through 'Indeed jobs' and I went for an agency as it said part time and minimum contract (I was planning to come back home for the summer to be with Kody anyway). This situation added more chaos to my stress and health.

42.   'Detox' 06.06.2023

Time to detox,
My health is in flux,
My energy feels drained,
I don't want to do much

Step 1, cleanse my mind,
Positive thinking I must find,
Words I think to myself must be kind.
Time to re-wind,
Reset my mind,
Make positive new connections,
What I want is to heal,
So positive thoughts I must be collecting.

Morning routine, ensure space for meditation,
Present moment awareness and positive affirmations,
Visualise myself as healthy, vibrant, and strong,
know my path is as it should be, there are no wrongs.
No time or space for doubts or negativity,
Ground myself with roots like the resilient oak tree,
Connect with Mother Earth and make offerings each day,

She can take away any disease and pain and show me another way.

Uplift myself, hold my head high, send my energetic light beam up to Father sky.

Be the clear channel between the two, I must try,

Be confident and courageous, so that I can thrive.

Step 2, take care and consideration to what I put in and on my body,

Toxins are everywhere, no more biscuits for me.

Cut out processed foods and eating to excess,

Regular times to eat so my body knows when to digest.

The Ayurvedic way has worked for me before,

Need to lower my 'vata' (air) and 'pita' (fire) element to open the healing door.

So, first need a complete detox and reset,

Mung bean soup- easy to digest.

Need to clear all the toxins so I can start afresh,

Healthy herbal teas and vitamins,

Give my body chance to rest.

Step 3, cleanse my space, and my energy,

Only allow people in my life who are good for me.

Not people who demand my trust and make me feel uncomfortable.

Not people who lie to me and make me feel small,

that just causes trouble.

Cleanse with sage, a salt bath, crystals and natural tobacco,

this will help my healing and keep my energy in flow.

Step 4, remove pressure I have self-imposed,

Know that I am great, no matter what I have to show,

Relax in the present moment,

allow self to be slow.

Trust the universe has always got me,

Spirit, mind, body head to toe.

Step 5, enjoy each day and live in gratitude,

The more good I choose to see,

The more good will come through.

Grateful each day I wake to a new day on this Earth.

Grateful that on my to do list, my wellbeing comes first.

Grateful for the lessons and learnings of this current time.

Grateful for the profound positive transformation of a lifetime.

Right now I am in mushy caterpillar stage,

So this is my time to visualise, the new me, blue butterfly,

a new dawn,

a new page.

43.   'Affirmations' 07.06.2023

I am happy, healthy, peaceful and safe.
I am strong, present, wealthy,
I radiate light in each day!

My body is perfect and functions great,
I live by divine timing,
No such thing as late!

The power of my mind is unstoppable,
My positive thoughts create many miracles.

Wealth and abundance flow to me easily,
I enjoy my work and am fulfilled,
I leave a legacy.

I am safe, I am protected, the universe always got me.
Angels, guides and God by my side, there is no stopping me.
I've got my own back,
my front and sides too,
Through any challenge I rise up and always get through.

I live a life of love, loving myself fully.

Amazing people surround me,

Unconditionally loving me.

I radiate gratitude and positivity,

I am a joy to have around,

Life in the party.

I am strongly connected with spirit,

I have magic abilities,

My intuition is spot on,

I follow it and trust where it leads me.

The universe got me, I am safe, I am well,

I live a life of adventure,

With many inspiring stories to tell.

44.   'Magic Wand' 08.06.2023

*Manifesting affirmations example: Saying what you
want to happen in the tense that it already happening*

I have a healthy, strong, beautiful, balanced

Mind, body and spirit.

I have an abundance of close connections,

Wealth, positivity, time.

I am trusting my gut and all my decisions.

I do fulfilling OT work with children and Autism.

I do healthy and strengthening daily routines- diet and practices-
I feel amazing every day!

I continue to give, receive, learn and teach, would not have it
another way.

I have my poems and spoken word recorded,

Connecting with people all over the world.

I have a published book- "The beautiful you" inspiring hearts,
offering comfort as this planet continues its twirl.

I have a Qi gong website and courses complete.

A preventative and sustainable healthcare intervention,
empowering people to their health complications beat.

I am leaving a legacy of my life,

Completing all soul missions,

Known as a ray of light.

45.　　'Young and free' 28.06.2023

This is actually a made-up song I sang to the tune of 'Let it be' by the Beatles for positive affirmations on a walk to help me during my time of ill health.

I am young and I am free,
I am as strong as the oak tree,
I'm living each day, to the full.
I can heal my body with my mind.

I am healthy, I am strong, I am wealthy, I live long,
A life full of adventure,
And love…

I have joy in each day,
wouldn't have it another way,
Each day is sacred,
On this Earth.
I love the feeling of the moon,
And the magic of each loon.
I feel gratitude for all that I go through,
As each and every challenge is a gift.

'cuz when we go through pain,
We are able to cleanse it away,
And become a butterfly…

We transform and we expand,
And we travel to different lands,
In this amazing,
Omni-verse.

We live life with joy and humour,
Because even the tragedy can be a healing comedy,
When we look at it through a 'funny, humour' lens.

46.   'Indigenous England' 11.07.2023

What are my roots and ancestral history,
Surely it is more than alcohol and TV?!...
Exploring other cultures has helped heal me,
Opening my mind and eyes to ancient practices,
allowing me to see.
To see, be free and just be me.
Connecting more with land, sky and sea.
There is so much magic in this life,
My interest now is to learn ancient English culture, I must try.

My understanding so far is that we are forest people,
Working with plants, trees and animals, seeing them as equal.
The UK used to be a huge forest on an island,
So our soil is full of roots which hold wisdom and guidance.

Working with the fairies and mythical creatures of the woods,
Witchcraft and wizardry, had to be hidden, protected by hoods.
Medicine for all ailment's is provided by Mother Earth.
These ancient teachings and practices we must find and re-birth.

The Romans came and cut the forests,
Seeing this as our 'religion',
They damaged our soul in the process,
Made us loose our direction.

Taking away the identity of our ancestors…
Now society is heavily based on alcohol for us instead to
connect with…

"Have fun,
Don't think".

I feel so at home and connected with the woods,
Bluebell season and thinking of fairies makes me feel so good.

I am ready to learn more, re-discover all that was lost,
We are the indigenous people of English land,
in that there is magic before the chaos,
I trust.

Despite the health challenge I was facing, I still wanted to attend the festivals I had committed to and to support a friend with transport.

This has been the year of the most festivals I have been too- all spiritual and no alcohol and healing by nature. However not enough sleep. I was still in pain and uncertainty, but my mental health had some FOMO and wanting to have fun to prevent the depression.

I made many wonderful connections and friends at these festivals.

A random fun experience happened in this summer of 2023, age 26. This was during my rock-bottom era, intense health challenges in physical, mental, emotional, spiritual…the whole of me.

At one of the spiritual festivals, a friend told me about a healer in London who he knows could help me. As he told me about him, my gut felt good, light and expansive. I felt a feeling of peace and joy. I trusted. However the only time he could see me was the next morning, and I did not know where I would stay the night. I thought I would just see how things pan out as to what I would do.

As I was carrying my stuff from the festival to my car, a man pulled up on the path next to me on an electric bike that looked like a motor bike, offering to help me carry my things. There were not many people still at the festival and I was a bit hot and bothered so was grateful for the offer of help. He suggested we take half the stuff and both ride on his motorbike to take it to my car, then both ride back to collect the rest of the stuff. I love riding motorbikes (first time with my dad, age 11) and thought wow, great, just my luck!

This man is an engineer in his 50's, who lives half his time in England and other time in Thailand. He creates the electric motorbike style bikes he was riding. A very interesting guy. As we continued talking, I mentioned the healer I was excited to meet and when he asked if I had somewhere to stay, I explained I was not exactly sure of my plan yet. He offered me to stay on his boat and that a couple from the festival were also coming to stay as they had a flight the next day. I could not believe my luck! I thought "thankyou universe- pulling through", supporting an easy path for me to follow in order to make it to the healer's session. I took his luggage for him in my car as he took the train with his bike and I set off for the postcode he gave me.

I was quite surprised to arrive in a very affluent area in London, right by the river Thames. Very central and very fancy! Not the quiet canal I was expecting. He arrived 30 mins after me, around 10pm and we met up with the couple on a doc on the Thames. The couple being there made me feel more at ease (not usually recommended to go on the boat of someone you only met a few hours before, alone, at night time).

A man on a small wooden motor boat holding a lantern pulled up. It was all so mysterious and Sherlock Holmes style it felt so like "what are the odds?!" haha. We chugged our way down the Thames until we stopped at a huge black and white striped boat (old war/ sailor ship or something). It was huge. In my mind I was like "no way am I staying at the zebra boat mansion?!". We climbed the ladder to get on the deck (it really is a huge boat). It was so cool inside- rustic interior, bike parts and bikes hanging up like art, plants, candles, cushions- a very cute and cosy and creative set up. He even gave us robes and slippers to put on! So random and luxurious. It made me laugh because earlier that day I was considering sleeping in my car or my festival tent and now I had ended up on the river Thames, in a zebra boat mansion, adorned in robe and slippers, cooking stir fry at 1am! We ate the stir fry on the roof and watched the stars. All nice vibes.

The next day I saw the healer and he helped me in many profound ways. So I was super grateful and trusting of the universe for this whole experience, as my gut feeling at the beginning indicated this was the right thing to do, giving me a strong, uplifting, high vibrational 'yes'.

This is the most important thing that I, that we all, learn to trust and listen to our gut, allowing it to influence our decisions. For example, seeing the best in people but ignoring off gut feelings, can result in pain, danger and fearful situations. I have experienced a fair few of these lessons too- some very close calls with bad intentioned people, but often I feel spirit protects me and guides me out of them, or gives me a lesson to learn, heal and expand my soul from.

Someone I told about the boat experience said I was an idiot and that I could have been locked in a room and had my "organs cut out and sold". This hit me deep and made me remember that not everyone has good intentions, a thought I did not fully consider when I got onto that boat.

However, it is also important not to shut down and develop trust issues and anxiety, which leads to poor wellbeing and being closed to good opportunities too.

So it really comes down to tuning into our gut, allowing it to be our compass, guided by Spirit. I am still learning to do this, I am by no means a pro, and part of my shadow is trusting too easily, allowing the good I see in people to override the red flags and warning signs, which can be perceived as Naïve and not seeing things fully for what they are.

As life is trying to teach me again and again...

The next poem was written following an unpleasant interaction with a 'festival friend'. I was unsure of sharing my experience of this as it is very personal… however I have chosen to share it as I am sure so many women can relate to this. Men too. You are not alone. I love you.

*Next page: Trigger warning: Sexual abuse
(To skip, go to pg 242.)

47.   'Express girl' 18.09.2023

Express girl, let it out
Its releasing to scream and shout,
What happened was wrong, without a doubt,
Cut his lips and his dick off,
To no other girl he shall pout.
Luring into his user trap,
Feeling used, abused, treated like crap,
Feeling invaded and disrespected,
Feeling unclean and neglected.

My sacred space entered, without my consent,
Cum ejaculated without care for consequence.
Easy for you, continuing your life as planned…
But for me anxiety and PTSD,
About what could and can.
Diseases and pregnancy on my mind…
the pregnancy termination destroyed me last time,
Promised myself I would never do that again,
So I am strict, always cover the end!

How did this happen,
I though he was my friend…

I felt like one of the lads,

On a London adventure,

Without need to fend.

When I broke down in tears and shock after,

He said "just go and take an emergency contraception".

Is he mad, what a cunt,

That pill is so toxic,

Already my womb is in crisis, you ignorant prick.

Externally I look fine, like I am okay,

But inside I am so damaged,

Physical, emotions and mentally.

Feeling alone in it, worried it was my own fault,

That feeling of weak broken boundaries, I feel I have guilt.

Confused though, as he had all the information of my no,

Yet he took me by surprise,

It happened so quick, my processing slow.

At least his true colours I now clearly know,

You are dead to me 'friend',

Wow you were an actor in a show.

Feeling silly for not seeing clearly,

Tired and exhausted and trusting too easily.

My invisible autism and slow processing I feel played a big part,

I don't always pick up on red flags, live life on the edge,

not always socially smart.

The doctors and nurses told me today,

That what happened was rape,

And I am not to blame.

They said most rape cases happen with someone you know,

Not down back alleys with an obvious foe,

Not always a clear enemy…

It's strange as I felt a connection…

but you must gain my consent before entering me!

I feel quite withdrawn, I don't want to connect with people,

I can't hide my feelings and don't want to share,

fear of no longer treated as equal.

Being misunderstood, would do more harm than good,

Being told all of the 'you should's'.

In hindsight it is clear, what I should have done,

Knocked him round the head one,

But in the moment, I froze.

In shock. Thoughts none.

BUT… I refuse to sink into victim mentality,

I am a warrior and as strong as the Oak tree,

Nothing can break me,

Instead, I become stronger, learning lessons, God sees.

First step- Detox and cleanse,

With green juice, salt baths, sage, qi gong, stretch and bend.

Clean foods, rest, time with me.

Writing, meditation,

Walks with Kody.

Self-time, self-care, self-love priority.

Heal myself- mind, spirit, body.

And integrate the learnings…

Don't cut out sleep so I am living exhausted,

Have energy to think, feel the vibes, no haunted!

Allow more processing time to make decisions,

Communicate with gut feelings in every instance.

See things and people clearly, don't just focus on the light,

Don't be so naive or too people pleasing to fight.

Write down my boundaries and read them each day,

So that in my processing there is no delay.

Practice saying 'no' to the things I don't want to do

And stick with that decision, don't be swayed or forced to.

Allow wind and rain to cleanse me,

Release negative energies to the Earth,

That do not belong in me.

Soak in healing light from the sun,

Allow self to re-birth.

Absorb the magic of the moon,

Especially to my womb.

Make prayers and affirmations,
Create a self-love energy cocoon.

Relax, let it go, take the lesson on the chin,
Bounce back up even stronger, wiser and smile a big grin.
Remember it's all a game,
life is quick,
sad times pass,
Use the experience to your advantage,
Learn and level up soul fast.

Trust that all is well,
Visualise self as happy, healthy and strong,
Always protected
and at one
with God.

48.   'The Wave and the Cave' 07.10.2023

The wave of life,
Up and down,
Triggering smiles and frowns-
A true merry go round!

What goes around comes around,
So seek no revenge,
Just keep giving out love,
Always and again.

One moment we're smiling, living life at the top,
Next moment the universe fish slaps us round the face
and for our tears we need a mop.

Aspects of life, crumbling like dominos,
When will it stop,
Maybe when we reach rock bottom,
Bottom rock.

From this place of darkness,

It's easy to become a cave,

Closing in on ourselves,

Cut contact,

Become our own doom and gloom slave.

Motivation lacking,

Self-care cracking,

Brain goes dead,

Thoughts jumbled,

Low moods stacking.

That's when we realise,

Alone in this self-cave,

It's just me, myself and I,

The only way is to go within- be brave.

Only the one present in this cave,

holds the keys to unlocking our healing

and be saved.

Talk to self in a mirror,

Don't grimace or snigger,

Lock eyes and see what colours and shapes glimmer.

Marvel at the beauty of an eye,

what a creation..

Also, the window into our soul,
The inner us so wise, so patient.

If we're going in, we may as well make it deep,
Show yourself and soul some love,
Open to universal secrets soul keeps.

Tell yourself how kind you are,
How strong, how sweet.
Absorb these kind words as truth,
And this true you, you shall meet.

Big yourself up, blow your own horn,
Be in love with yourself and be truly adored.
Envision at your core a bright beautiful light,
Lighting up your cave,
Clearing out anxieties and freights.
With this self-love and light within us,
Our core strong,
Nothing sways our peace.
It doesn't matter what the external world brings,
We will just sway in the breeze, peaceful leaf.

Swaying in life's breezes,
Riding life's flow,
The up and down rollercoaster,
I know you know.

We can still go for the ride,
Just maintain our peace within,
Accept the dark times when they come,
But don't allow negativity to creep in.

To maintain this approach means challenging
times pass quicker,
Keep our energy in trust and life will match us,
good times delivered.

We can choose to have a smoother ride,
play safe, stick to our routine...
Or we can choose to live life on the edge,
More adventures come with more screams.

For me the latter matches my life,
and I am grateful for the intensity,
Many funny stories to tell,
And bruises and scars a plenty.

I choose an adventurous life,
less stability but more freedom,
So, I will remember this poem to remind me of the light inside
my cave,

Peaceful Centre,

Shining Temple,

Inner Kingdom.

49.   'I Give Thanks' 16.10.2023

I give thanks for the magnificent sky,
Stars rainbows and clouds fill my eyes.
I give thanks to the Most High,
Blessing my life journey,
Guiding my steps,
Each experience keeping me on my toes learning.

I give thanks to the Earth which holds me,
Witnessing all the mysteries,
Magic whispering through the trees.

I give thanks for the challenges,
none of them will break me,
I am a warrior of light,
I am stable, yet I am free.

I give thanks for this life,
I will use it wisely,
I already am,
Spirit guides me.

I give thanks for the opportunity to help another smile,

Make a difference,

To spread strong and loving gentleness in every instance.

I give thanks for all the magic in my life so far,

I've seen many shooting stars,

Had many moments of 'a-ha's!'

I give thanks for the blessed situation that I live,

Grateful for all the fun and inspiration I have now,

and have already lived.

Using this gratitude to propel me always,

Out into the world in the sun,

Storms,

and breezy shade.

50.   'How do I feel' 26.10.2023

How do I feel?...

I feel peaceful.
I feel present in the moment,
Calm and blissful.
I feel gratitude and connection with my senses,
The setting sun shines on my face,
The tweeting birds fill my ears with grace.

I feel slightly overwhelmed by all that I must do.
I know I need to keep my energy good and dream a dream to come true.
I need to trust and be open,
Knowing that Spirit knows what's best for me,
Always carving my path,
To me a mystery,
All trust, as no see.

***

The Autumn and Winter I continued my healing, working with my affirmations, an interesting healer I met, self-care and daily practices. I had lots of time in the woods with Kody, continued working and had a lot of time at home. My health physically was improving. My balance in everything I was gradually regaining.

It took a while, but I forgive.

Everyone makes mistakes or may misread situations…

And holding grudges, hurt, anger… only hurts ourselves.

I choose to learn from the lesson and heal.

Life goes on. And I am alive today…thankyou!

***

In January I am setting off with my sister for an adventure in Central America, something I have always wanted to do. The reason for this travel, is to get it out of my system, fulfil that soul desire, so that I can then return to the UK and be more settled and prioritise Kody. He is the centre of my world. The plan is to use my savings to buy a van for me and Kody to explore the UK, being together every day for approximately the next 5-6 years (his life expectancy). I want to give him all of my attention as he is my bestest friend and the biggest love of my life.

Right now, adventure awaits!

Central America Travel, Journal entry 04.03.2024

Well, what a crazy time.

I am currently in Central America in Panama. I have been travelling since the 3rd of January (2 months) and have been to Costa Rica and Panama. I need to write to help process some of the events of the past week in particular, but also the travel as a whole.

It is a life changing and transformative, fun and adventurous, as well as challenging experience. As always, life is intense.

The first three weeks I was with my sister Laura in Costa Rica. We visited many places, went to lots of national parks, did many adventurous experiences (white water rafting, hiking a volcano, La Salta rope swing, 12000 ft skydive, cacao farm tours, horseback riding, the cloud forest, ziplining, Tarzan swing 50ft drop, quad bike riding, surfing and dancing!). It was a beautiful time and Laura planned it all so well, with her excel spreadsheet (!) to make the most of the time she had. It was great and we made memories to last a lifetime. We stayed in beautiful places in interesting and diverse locations and met many great people along the way. Laura and I have a deep bond. We have our differences but that is where we learn from each other. We have unconditional love and the sister bond is forever strong. I love her so much. She is a Sagittarius moon like me, connecting over our love of adventure.

***

One time on a beach at midnight I was riding the back of a quad bike of a local guy I just met on a beach, Carribean side of Costa Rica. There were literally red flags up and blowing in the wind all along the beach (weather warning) and my gut was so off. Especially as I thought we were just going to drive down the busy beach high street, where lots of people were, yet he drove out of town and took me to another beach where he proceeded to drive full speed over the sand dunes in the full moon light (this was a little epic at least).

However, when I saw the beach sign, I realised this was the beach I had seen on Google maps- where a couple had left a review that they were mugged by guys with machetes who were hiding in the jungle on this beach. As all this was processing in my head and I was seeing the literal red flags, I thought, "oh no this is really bad, I am about to be cut up by machetes and this will be my death".

I managed to speak up and demand we go back and after I said this twice, he did turn around. Phew a bit of relief that he listened to me at least. He stopped by the road but still on the beach and I had a moment to calm down my panic and stand away from him. He then shared with me that his mum passed away the year before and he began crying, still heavily grieving. I felt a bit bad then for thinking he was going to kill me and thought ah maybe my thoughts are being dramatic.

He dropped me back to my hostel and said we could go and see waterfalls on the quadbike the next day. I thought okay cool. What a nice opportunity!

However gut feelings are never wrong and I should have listened to the red flags I was seeing, and not been overridden by my curiosity and love of adventure and new experiences.

Some parts were nice and felt like a nice friendship (I made friendship vibe very clear from the beginning) but then he began getting overly in my space and was getting angry that I did not want to connect with him in that way. I was in a terrible location... In the middle of the mountains/ jungle, alone with this guy, who had took me here on the way back from the waterfalls to show me his project (he was building a huge house with lookout platform (I was intrigued by the lookout platform).

It was like he would flip between throwing my shoes at me and calling me a bitch to then grabbing me and trying to kiss me to the point where I was pushing him away. It was getting more intense as he would slap my bum and ignore me telling him to stop and was trying to put me against the wall. I did panic and thought in this moment, "ah sh*t, the red flags!" I am an idiot for letting my understanding of grief override the clear signs of danger I was being given.

I was preparing myself for things to escalate and I was in a state of fight or flight, when my saviour (this guy's friend) arrived at the location and came onto the platform as the guy slapped my bum again and the friend witnessed me tell him to stop touching me and the friend was like "what are you doing?" and then to me "are you okay?" which was my chance to say no I am not okay and I want to go back to the town. It all worked out okay (thanks to this guys friend) but it was a close call. I think perhaps he would benefit from mental health support as the switch would happen in seconds and he felt quite unstable, a very big strong man too, with a lot of anger, likely partially stemming from the pain of his grief. He seemed desperate for connection, indicating loneliness and sadness, and my heart goes out to him hoping he will find his healing and his happiness again.

This experience was another reminder to myself to not be so blinded by the light that you miss the dark and the danger and the bad intentions. I am grateful that I got out of that lesson alive and well… it could have gone west for sure.

Have you ever had experiences like this?

Where you trust too easily, see only the good and then either get hurt, taken advantage of or let down?

And then feel silly for getting in the situation, as with hindsight danger is clear, and you then feel dissuaded from telling close ones what you experienced?

It is good to reflect. Life is a balance of being open and trusting, but listening to gut feeling above all else and using discernment to keep ourselves safe. I continue my learning. I realise I have, on many occasions, trusted too easily and put myself in isolated and risky situations without realising.

I realise I have been lucky to receive Spirit's protection in such times.

I am now more aware in keeping myself safe and tuning into my gut to guide me. I invite you to begin or continue to connect with your gut feeling with regards to decisions, people, environments and situations. It is always trying to keep us safe and is for our highest good. It is said that our Spirit Guide's heart lives within our gut and it is them who is guiding us, next to our higher self.

***

Laura was with me in Bocas Del Toro (Caribbean Island in Panama) for her last three days. We stayed on the quiet side of the island and went to bed early, woke up early, relaxed, rested and went on a beautiful tour to Zapatilla island- the most beautiful beach I have ever experienced. On the tour we also saw a dolphin mother with her calf, and they were playing in the waves of the boat. It was a breathtaking moment. I feel very connected with the spirit of the dolphin and their playful, joyful energy, riding the waves of life.

Laura left for England as she had to return to work. I waved her off and then was like "hmm, what now?" ...

I decided to go and have an ice cream and sit by the sea. I felt a bit flat and lost at first as I had not planned further than where I would stay that night. I decided I needed an adventure and messaged my friend who was our tour guide from the Dolphin tour. He suggested going out on a Jet Ski experience with him from his tour company (mates rates applied) and I thought why not, adrenaline will kick me into action. It was a great adventure, and we went very far and very fast, to starfish beach where we swam with snorkels and saw so many huge red starfish under the clear water (they looked like Pokémon). So beautiful! Then I had a go driving the jet ski and went up to 45 mph and no crashes!

It worked and brought me back to excitement and curiosity for the travel. That night I met with my friend, Destiny, who I had met previously in Costa Rica. We connected so beautifully! She is such a divine and intuitive woman, and we really understand each other on a very deep and loving level. We had a beautiful night of dancing at Barco Hundido on Thursday Reggae night (best night out!) and I really expressed myself with my dancing. Medicine through movement!

Destiny left the next day, and I had planned to just stay two more nights. However, this turned into one month! I really got into dancing, and it felt very healing for me. I did go through a couple of weeks of bad habits, teenage me returning, drinking and up all night!

However, this is not me now so I managed to enjoy that time but then care about my health again and would be there with my 2L bottle of water, dancing and having a very intense workout in the process, therefore sweating LOTS (it's the Caribbean baby) and hydrating.

I enjoyed the island's sense of community and made friends with many locals. I think this is why I stayed (also as I had never made a clear plan to leave). I started doing some boxing training with a friend who I made. He had a dog too who was great as I missed Kody so much, so it was nice to have a dog connection and thoughts of Kody, connecting with him through the spirit of the dog. His dog followed me everywhere, whenever I walked around the town. It was so cute.

This man, Donatello, invited me to stay at his home and meet his family and I accepted. It was a great authentic experience. Basic living- a wooden hut with no power or running water. The only downside to this was when I had a tummy bug (aka the sh*ts which turned out to be a form of E. coli!) so needed to speed walk to the cafe in the mornings (crying and laughing at this), the heat, and the mosquitos. However, the mosquitos we combated with the spiral incense which burns and works extremely well! The sh*ts subsided with medication (after attending a doctor after 1 week of being very unwell and not realising how severe it was!) which solved that problem. For the heat I had the use of a handheld fan which I got for $2.95 (I love this fan!) and we used collected cool rainwater from the bucket to wash and feel fresh. The benefits of this experience were deep.

We do not need luxury to be happy. The love and generosity he shared to me was inspiring and so gratefully received. He shared everything. He is so present, free, determined, focused, generous, kind and funny. An impressive Boxer and I see a bright and abundant future for him.

Bocas del Toro is interesting because everything is so expensive, like the same prices as in the UK and with many things more expensive, however the living wage is minimal. People work a lot yet do not get paid well, considering the price of living. It seems like a trap, which maintains a poverty cycle. Yet what was also affirmed to me is that those with less material possessions and items, are, in many cases, more generous, happy, present and free.

This month was great in so many ways, I had good experiences and met some awesome people (big up Maria from Berlin) and felt part of a community. I had my nose re-pierced and two new tattoos. A cosmic Dolphin tattoo (see above my connection with dolphins) and unplanned, the next day, a tattoo of Kody at the top of my arm, adding to the 'picture map' (now looking like a tattoo sleeve!) of my understanding of life. Kody is at the top above the lotus flower as he represents pure unconditional love, which is the essence of enlightenment. Many fun memories made during this time.

However, I also felt like I slipped into some unhealthy habits in the process. As I was out late dancing (although no more alcohol at this point), I woke up late in the heat and then it was too hot to do my morning routines (workout, Qi Gong) and I wanted to make the most of the day and adventure to a beach or somewhere.

By now, we all know what happens when I slip out of and do not prioritise my morning routine and self-care. I felt like I was not being very productive either working on my projects, seeing new places or earning money. I felt quite directionless and stuck, and I did not know why. I felt my energy depleted and felt somewhat trapped, unable to move forwards. As a result, my emotions became heavier. I was tired from not getting enough sleep and ill after having bad water/ E. coli.

Interestingly, it appears (as always does eventually), that there was a reason for my extended stay in Bocas Del Toro.

I met a Panamanian man, Harold, who I connected with over a conversation about star signs. He is an astrologer and has much insight and understanding into star signs and spirituality. It was a very interesting conversation. He explained that because in my chart I have Pluto in Sagittarius in the 1st house, that my life this time round is full of challenges to break me down and test me to rise up from the ashes (an insight I added to 'My Avatar' at the beginning). I was like damn, that really explains all the consistent intense experiences I have had through my life. I always bounce back though. Always stronger than before.

Harold interested me a lot, and although only 21, he has much insight and wisdom and teaches his knowledge well. He also works with the plant medicine of Ayahuasca. This is something I had not experienced before now. I have had some opportunities before, but I did not feel the calling and knew that I would know if and when the time was right. This was that time. The fact that we were friends first and then shared deep spiritual conversations, I trusted him, and felt relaxed in his presence, all indicated to me that the universe was showing me my next step.

Donatello and I travelled to Boquete in mainland Panama to stay up in the mountains with our friend Angel who we met in Bocas Del Toro. We were later joined by Maria. It was cute, the four of us all had a sleepover in Angel's room. We shared food, Cacao, walks, and time. Great people. Angel has an amazing dog too!

However, this week I felt extremely down and low and was confused as to why. It was a crazy intense feeling with no clear origin. However, in retrospect this is now clear and was my intuition (read on...).

At the end of the few days, I went to meet Harold at a sweet bungalow in the nature of the mountains. It was so beautiful. This was the setting for my first Ayahuasca ceremony, 1:1. A powerful and profound plant medicine, an intense and transformative experience. I fasted all day, aside from some initial fruit when I woke up and prepared during the day by doing Qi Gong, meditation, Sage cleanse, writing and intention setting. I had been following the 'dieta' all week of no meat, caffeine, sugar, alcohol etc. I felt calm and ready. I trusted.

It was a beautiful experience. I felt joyful, curious, in awe. I had many realisations and clarity for my intentions. We watched the stars, meditated, danced, surrendered, sang, were still, did Qi Gong and had many downloads of understanding.

I had a clarity and understanding of my own patterns and unhealthy attachment styles. It appears I have been acting in response to 'abandonment issues'. Even though my rational mind knows I am not abandoned, my emotional self was feeling it this way. My father and mother breaking up when I was three, Jim dying, relationships and other life events, have had the impact on my emotional self of feeling abandoned. I expressed this with Harold who told me that it is likely when I get into relationships, I may lose myself, not taking care of myself with a subconscious (un)truth that people will only stay if I need looking after. Therefore, I stop taking care of myself and doing the things I enjoy, becoming absorbed into the other person to make the most of the connection before they 'leave' (subconscious fear). This then causes them to fall out of love with me and then leave…. Starting the feeling of abandonment and the cycle again. It was so interesting as in my logical mind I know I was never abandoned and things happen as it is life, part of the experience, and new doors are opening all the time… for example I have a wide family due to parent remarriages and met many amazing people as a result. However my emotional self was not aligned with this, and felt like a hurt child.

This is why I have often thought and felt that I am better off on my own, as when I am on my own, I feel balanced and happy, as I am doing all the things that give me joy and good wellbeing. This was so clear, and now I am aware of this subconscious pattern, I can change it. Keep myself as me, prioritise my morning routines, have plans and goals and stick to them. Be okay on my own but open to connect with others, and to make peace with the inevitable impermanence of everything. Connection, not attachment.

Most people in some way or another experience this fear of abandonment so we can support each other to understand and work through this. Remember, even if the rational thinking mind feels secure and can make sense of why people come in and out of our life, sometimes our emotional body needs more care and attention throughout this process.

At one point of the ceremony, I had an intense emotional breakdown. This was following a thought of Kody. I felt such emotional pain missing him and I was crying intensely and my body contracting in sadness. I felt so far from him, and I suddenly knew I wanted to be at home with him. I wanted to cut my travel short and return to him as he is the most important being in my life and we are one and I did not want to be far from him. I was saying sorry to him a lot and felt this experience gave me the clarity I needed for what comes next with my travel. It was a very intense feeling of grief, coupled with a feeling of guilt. I knew I must get back to him.

The ceremony ended beautifully with singing, gratitude and grapes. The stars were unbelievable. This experience lifted the depression I had been feeling and I felt I was powerful, strong and full of love and clarity. I went back to Bocas Del Toro, shared my learning and experience with Donatello and Maria, and began looking at flights to the UK.

***

***

Two days later, the biggest shock and trauma of my life occurred.

Kody died.

I woke up to my phone vibrating from a call. I looked and I had missed calls from my mum and a message saying that she had bad news and could I have someone with me. I answered the next call, and she told me she had bad news. I thought to myself, as long as it is nothing to do with Kody, I will be okay.

However, this was like a premonition. I knew it would be linked to Kody before she even spoke. She explained that in the morning Kody had not been himself and she took him to the vet to have a check-up. The days leading up to this he had appeared happy and as normal, long walks, river playing, doing the morning farm chores.

The vet then called her and said he urgently needed to be put down as he had a tumour in his artery which had burst the artery and was causing internal bleeding and would be soon affecting his heart and breathing which may cause him to panic. My mum said she and my stepdad would video call me shortly, so that I could say goodbye to him. They were shocked too, as Kody had not displayed any signs of pain or discomfort, I even checked with mum following my ceremony.

After that initial phone call, I had a breakdown of shock and horror. The worst thing that could happen, my worst fear, coming true. Kody, my light, my love, my best friend, dying whilst I am away- finally on this trip, and before we could spend that precious time together that I have dreamed of for years. I hated myself for leaving. For not being there in his last moments. Fearing that he thought I had abandoned him. These intense emotions led me to bang my head repetitively with force on the window ledge, until Donatello caught my head and stopped me. I pulled myself together and answered the call from my mum and saw Kody at the vets. I spoke with the vet saying surely there is something she could do, and she explained that there is nothing at this stage and even a human would not be operated on.

I saw Kody and he appeared calm and had a waggy tail. I spoke with him; told him I was sorry, and I thanked him for the tremendous difference he made in my life and all the healing he brought me and everyone who met him. I told him how much I loved him and how much he had saved me. It was such a challenge to fight back the tears to try to sound calm for him. I told him we would always be together because our bond is so strong, and our souls are one.

I then sang 'Let it be' to him whilst he was put down, held and cuddled by my mum and my stepdad and wrapped in my hoodie. The call ended, and I was consumed by intense emotions of guilt, shame, shock, disbelief, non-acceptance, denial, depression and the tears and crying were so intense. I'm talking dribbling, mouth open, full on ugly cry. My eyes quickly became swollen and purple.

***

Later that day, my mum messaged an image of Kody's body in a blanket, and she had laid him to rest in his favourite places; the garden sunshine, by the oak tree and finally in the conservatory- my healing room where Kody and I spent many hours and many ceremonies. At my request she wrapped him in my unicorn blanket and found my favourite turquoise orgonite necklace to give him. This was to give his soul protection and love and to connect us as I have the black and white one with me on this travel. My mum made a beautiful ceremony space, lighting candles, conducting a sage ceremony for him and having all my spiritual items and tools around him. She called me and together we did a ceremony with him, singing healing chants and mum using my shamanic drum and singing bowl around him.

It was so sad but felt beautiful and made me feel connected and we did this for over one hour. His body spent the night in that space and mum sat with him for hours. She explained they would bury him the next day, next to the big oak tree and we would have a ceremonial send off and celebrate his life. So, for this, in the midst of my shock and denial, that same day I wrote a poem for Kody, and I have included this in its raw form.

51. 'Dear Kody' 26.02.2024

I can't believe the day has come,
You have left this Earth and flew.
The centre of my world, my love, my joy,
Kody, that is you.

I had so many plans for us in the years
I thought we had to come,
Living in a van, going to the sea,
More adventures to be won.

I wanted to be with you fully, give you all of my attention,
I'm so sorry you were so patiently waiting…
I think about you every moment,
even when I've not been near,
You are in my heart lighting the way each day,
by my side your footsteps I hear.

I thank you for your being,
you taught me about life.
You taught presence, joy and happiness,
which you held in every stride.

You are my best friend, the biggest love of my life,
my baby boy always...
I shall continue to spread your energy in each day that I rise.

The world was a better place because you were here on it;
so sweet, so pure, so innocent, enlightened soul,
teaching all how to unconditionally love and how to live.

Live happy, be free,
Be kind to everybody.
Find a game in everything,
It's about the play and not the win.

I have faith that we are still connected between the dimensions
I send prayers, songs, love and good intentions.

You are part of me as I am part of you,
Our energy fields integrated, together we will thrive,
...You and I
I'll be in this world and you'll be here in spirit,
I am with you too wherever you are,
always believe it.
And now you can come on every journey with me,
seeing different lands overseas.

Dream team always,

Walking the path of existence together in this life,

and all the next.

I will try to make you proud,

I will do my best.

I send you so much gratitude, blessings, love and cuddles

I thank you a million times thankyou, thankyou, thankyou,

You made my life special.

The best companion and friend,

My love for you is infinite and it will never end.

Now be free, spread your wings,

See what the Great Spirit's next adventures bring

Keep me in your heart and feel the strength of love which sings,

I send you love and blessings every moment,

you are my favourite ever being.

Know my love will carry you and guide you

where your soul goes,

we are connected forever and always,

and I will see you again my best friend,

this is something I know.

Love you Kody AHO

***

The next morning, I woke up at 7am and walked to a restaurant to get good Wi-Fi. Donatello's dog followed me as usual and three other street dogs joined us on the way. I arrived at the restaurant with four dogs in total and it felt so profound, as I did not encourage any of them, but clearly, I had the spirit of the dog with me. I joined the video call with my family and our neighbour for Kody's ceremony. It was so sad yet so beautiful. My sister shared memories, Mum and Granny shared words and I shared my poem.

We celebrated the magnificent being that he is and expressed our gratitude and, of course, many tears were shed, and it was hard to hold it together at times due to the shock of it all. We had chosen music to be played in between on a playlist we had made. Music included: All of me- John Legend, I love you- Billie Eilish, Everglow- Coldplay, Oak Tree - Lua Maria, Adrian Freedman, spiritual songs which Kody always tolerated me playing on repeat (Pachamama and faiths hymn- Beautiful Chorus) and to celebrate Kody's impact in the world, Positive Vibration- Bob Marley.

They carried him under the Oak tree and buried him with his favourite blanket and toys, my turquoise orgonite necklace and my lilac purple spiritual scarf and a Cacao offering.

What followed for me was days of paralysis, grief, reckless thoughts, feeling extreme, feeling numb, feeling dead inside and wearing sunglasses to hide my swollen eyes and a hat to hide the lump on my forehead from the headbanging. I felt lifeless. My world shattered. Me and Kody are so connected, we are the same. I feel that the best part of me is Kody. And now Kody is dead, the best part of me, dead. The guilt, the shame, the denial. This is the most challenging grief for me yet. Grief is strange because you are somewhat helpless. You cannot change it. It is beyond our control. Which can make it a very challenging pain. I knew I was attached to Kody and clearly the universe is trying to teach me about non-attachment. In the harshest, most 'fish slap around the face' way possible.

I know that death is as natural as life, and it is to be embraced and celebrated. I know that death is not the end of everything and that the soul is eternal and expands and transforms but never dies. I know we can still connect with those loved ones who have passed over through our thoughts, intentions and prayers and that we can tune in to feel their energy. I know that they can be angels and guides for us and continue to support and love us.

Yet still, knowing that in this lifetime I will never again touch his beautiful soft fur, look deeply into his loving brown eyes or have those morning cuddles, hits so deep. Yet I must be strong and send him love and be able to let go, allowing his spirit to fly as I do not want him to feel constrained or trapped by my inability to let go. The greater the pain mirrors the greatness of the love.

This is my biggest pain, as it is my greatest love.

But oh, how grateful am I to have experienced love like this at all. As they say, it is better to have loved and lost than never have loved at all.

All how I had been feeling the previous week now made sense- the unexplained depression in Boquete and what I felt in the ceremony… all signs. Also, what are the odds that two weeks before Kody died, I got his face tattooed on my arm- something I have thought for years but literally now just done? Somehow, my spirit was preparing me for this loss.

One day I woke up and just needed to escape to nature. I felt so on edge and just needed to find space and cry. Donatello was half asleep and I told him I was going to a beach and for him to have a nice day, as I did not think I would see him for the rest of the day. I walked 30 minutes to a beach, one of the dogs came with me <3, and found a bench amongst the trees in the shade. I lay down on it, put my headphones in and cried and cried and cried. About an hour later I heard a noise, so I opened my eyes and to my surprise, there was Donatello with his cousin's motorbike. He actually came and found me, even though I had been so vague and not expected to see him (assigning myself to a day of solitude and loneliness). He said come on; we're going on an adventure to the blue lagoon. This gave me a pleasant lift and it made me smile that he did this, bringing a bit of sparkle to my dark night.

We went up to the blue lagoon, riding through the jungle. Aware that I was in a mode where I needed to feel something intense e.g. adrenaline, to counteract the feeling of wanting to die, Donatello gave me experiences which did just that (some crazy off road motorbiking through the jungle and he told me to hold my arms out and close my eyes and trust (I was passenger, not driving lol).

We had been to the lagoon before but never swam as it is very secluded and although beautiful, you cannot see into it and it is very deep and connected to the wide-open ocean, a seemingly perfect home for sharks or Caiman. How I was feeling I had lost care. I thought Kody is brave and fearless so I should be too. If there is a shark or something in there that will eat me, then it is my time to die too, and I will join Kody. I jumped off a tree branch into the lagoon and waited about 20 seconds. Nothing ate me. I survived. So, I was like, okay, today is not my day to die, then panicked and quickly got out. My mind so crazy.

That evening we walked past the airport and saw two helicopters. Again, tuning into me, Donatello asked me if I wanted to do something crazy. I was like "sure". Low and behold the helicopter doors opened. We got inside (the dog too), closed the door and mimed pretended to fly (didn't actually touch anything). The adrenaline of knowing we could be arrested if we were caught helped me feel alive. Silly really but it did give me a lift of excitement, and the mission was completed successfully. Panama is a very strict country and we would have been in biiiiig trouble if caught. Oh, the adrenaline of potentially ruining my life fuelled me so much at this time… if that gives any insight into my mental state (In my right mind I would never do this).

The focus of my days was to breathe, drink water and try and have fruit. It was the bare minimum of self-care but felt like the maximum. I made my phone lock screen a simple self-care to do list and images of Kody to motivate me to do these things as he would want me to. One night I was in the hammock, with my music and crying a lot. Donatello came and got in behind me, hugged me and swayed the hammock. We stayed like that for hours and I released many tears. It also touched me greatly how discreetly, Donatello shed some tears too. I knew he was really feeling me… sharing my pain. It was profound and beautiful. It makes sense that I was 'stuck' on the island- it was essential I had friends around me during this time, can you imagine if I was alone in a random hostel in Central America with no support?...

What was so crazy is that I randomly saw a friend, Alice, from high school passing in the street on this island?! She was there for one night only and we just so happened to cross paths. I have not seen her in years (about 10!), but to spend time with her, a piece of home, on the day of Kody's death was very profound and divinely orchestrated. Grateful for this unlikely meeting.

I felt like my emotional body had been hit by a truck, invisibly destroyed and paralysed, like a physical body would be seen with the same impact. I felt like I had died inside. Life felt meaningless. My biggest love and joy is gone. My plans are foiled (once again… universe must be teaching me not to make plans? Or at least do not be attached to them...). My motivation and sense of home dissolved.

Now I know so many people reading this can relate to this feeling.

52.　　'Pain Paralysis' 07.03.2024

In life we will experience great pain,
This can happen in many ways, and will come again and again.

The pain can affect us using different tactics,
It could come as an injury, accident, a bee sting on your lip.
It could come as a broken leg, disease,
or physical body out of sync.

It could come as stressful thoughts, overwhelm,
choked in a invisible negativity bind
It could come as someone you meet being unkind,
It could come as thoughts of suicide on your mind,
It could come from an empathetic heart,
Feeling all the suffering of mankind.

Feeling the pain of places there is conflict,
hearts breaking for families that need love but are out of physical reach.
Feeling the pain of Mother Earth, choked lungs, massacred trees, polluted waters,
plastic covering the beach.

Sometimes we can experience Pain Paralysis,

The pain is too much, and it is difficult to shift.

We may be unable to move physically our bodies,

We may be unable to see any light that each day brings.

We may be so full of emotions we detach from ourselves,

Or we may explode like a volcano cloud,

Fearful, aggressive, loud.

We may lose our motivation for everything,

Hard to be productive, or enjoy leisure,

Self-care in the bin.

When this happens, know you are not alone.

Many have experienced and overcome this,

in the worlds community this is shown.

Which means you can do it too, have faith,

Trust flowing through your bones.

Be open to possibilities and tools,

don't give up hope.

Keep your spirit strong,

it is unbreakable when you put that intention in.

Trust that the pain has come to serve you as a gift,

There is a lesson in every experience,

When we train ourselves to see it.

For pain is necessary for transformation to take place,

Without it we would never level up or expand in this life game.

Now that would be boring, to always stay the same,

So thank you pain, as it's from you that more strength is gained,

When you push me to my limits, it drives me insane,

It forces me to dig deep within,

in search of how to be saved.

It's there I find love again,

at the centre of my being,

It reminds me to breathe, drink water, be gentle

and proud of even doing the minimum.

It gives a warm tingly feeling inside,

it reminds me to trust and enjoy the ride.

Each time I visit this depth in my centre,

I re-emerge lighter and stronger than ever,

I know I am resilient to what life throws.

I may go down to the depths,

but I will always bounce back up again,

God knows.

I feel much guilt when thinking of Kody and all the places we had not made it to yet, all the experiences yet to be had. I embrace and immerse myself in this intense heavy feeling, so it can be acknowledged, processed and give me wisdom going forwards.

I am sure many people can relate to feelings of guilt, which we can experience for a variety of reasons- what we did, what we did not do, what we could have done differently.

The next poem lets really dive deep into that guilt feeling; face it head on, so it can then be transformed into love, to propel us forwards, guiding our present and future actions to be ever more compassionate and wise.

53.   'Guilt' 08.03.2024

The emotion that cuts deep
Keeps you up at night,
Disturbs sleep.

Complex guilt,
From where self-loathing is built,
Regrets of what's been and gone,
What we did…
or what we 'could've, should've' done.

Like a boulder, smashing into the heart,
And that's just the start,
Internal energy diminishing sharp.
Some things we have the power to change,
but some things we can't.

Allow the guilt to be felt,
To be acknowledged, processed,
This must be done in order to make progress.
It can happen that we will beat ourselves up,
But you must be gentle and not drain your own cup.
Instead, patch the holes and fill that baby up!

Think how you would speak to your best friend, your child,
With kindness and care,
To the one you love most in this life…
You would be understanding,
Non-judgemental and fair.
Speak to yourself with this same approach,
Inside we can keep an atmosphere of unconditional love and care.

From this state we can learn from the situation,
So we don't make the same mistake…
Instead gaining wisdom
and cultivating kindness to share.
Don't resort to self-hate and despair.

The world can beat us down,
No need to add to our reason to frown,
Prolonged internal negative feelings cause us to emotionally drown.
Instead forgive self and see if you can turn the situation around.
Do more good actions to make up for wrong doings
by which you feel defined by and bound,
Life is short, you can do good,
the world continues twirling round and round.
So, focus on what good you can do from today,
this moment, now.

It is said the Bach flower 'Pine' helps heal our guilt,

That natural 'Honey' aids forgiveness,

to help self-love to be rebuilt.

From this state of self-love,

we have the power to right our wrongs,

Either to the direct situation,

Or if not possible, pay it forward,

sing the world your love song.

Appreciate each moment with loved ones who are here,

One day they won't be and we'll regret any disagreements and fear,

And any time we are not being fully present with who we hold dear.

Learn from all situations and they are not wasted,

Top up your wisdom, don't displace it,

From the dark to the light, you can shapeshift,

Your life experience is the perspective from which you take it.

***

At the end of the week, I left the island and travelled to Chiriqui for my second Ayahuasca ceremony with my friend. This was already planned prior to Kody's death, and I felt that the timing of everything seemed to be for a reason. I decided to trust and step into this experience. I felt I had nothing to lose, as wanting to die was a thought taking over my mind.

For previous medicine experiences I have always prepared my mind and body well with meditation, affirmations, positive intentions and would never engage when I have been at my lowest points. I always have made it my challenge to save myself without anything external, to re-find my inner strength and re-claim my inner power and kingdom before engaging in any medicine ceremony. But this time was different...

I felt dead inside, like my soul had shattered and my motivation to rise up again was diminished. Kody is not just a dog, but my best friend, my baby, my teacher, my whole world. Love so unconditional and pure. The feeling of losing the being you love most is a hard pain, which many can relate to. So you know this hurt so deep. Therefore, I was not in my right mind. Medicines are powerful and it is always best to connect with them from a calm and stable peace of mind, getting our vibration high first through our own practices and preparation is so important.

That being said, for me, this experience, guided to by my gut, was profound, painful, scary and powerful, but actually, in the end, it saved me...

Holy sh*t the ceremony was intense. Now I am writing this, two days after that experience. Still very fresh.

It began with a feeling of gratitude and peace, yet I also felt emotionless. Later, the intense crying began. I was curled up in a ball, face on the grass. The ugly cry was back and I was in pure denial, repetitively saying 'no, no, no, no', calling Kody's name and crying like a desperate young child. I felt broken. I was broken. The feeling of wanting to die became so strong and overwhelming.

My spirit is strong to fight this and be good, however, I did not want to. I had no motivation.

I wanted to die and be with Kody so badly.

But a small part of me did not want that.

Laying on my back facing the stars seeming lifeless, I was talking with myself in my mind...

There was a conversation going on, the part of me who wanted to die, vs the part of me acknowledging those feelings and the pain but telling me not to give up, even though I wanted to. This battle with myself went on for what seemed a very long time. At one point I decided to just pretend to be dead and see what happened. I let go and was lifeless and blank, trying to encourage my soul to leave my body and go up to the stars.

Then something profound happened.

I saw around me large native American indigenous beings smiling at me, giving me healing, playing instruments over me. I suddenly felt not alone. At first, I was thinking, "wait but I am trying to die, don't heal me..." but then I had eye contact with one, felt pure love and care so did not resist and gave him a thankyou and surrendered to the healing.

One of them became Tlilik Tekuani, clear as anything, and he was playing his didgeridoo over me, as he has done in person many times. It was so clear. I felt loved and supported. I decided it is not my time to die yet. Not yet. Kody wants me to live. I felt him strongly in my memories and when I thought of these, his energy was with me strong and a clear message came through, that he is always with me now, on all my adventures and he wants me to really live. Live wild and free and not an ordinary life. Live to the fullest. Really LIVE. I made this decision and affirmed it 100 times. I choose to live. I choose life. Finally, that became clear and all of me was in agreement.

What happened next was a huge test. Suddenly I became extremely thirsty, a thirst of extremes I had not experienced before. My brain felt shrivelled, my organs hurt, my mouth was completely dry. It made me feel fear and panic and I was desperate for water. My friend brought me water and I gratefully drank from the cup. It was very difficult and painful to swallow. I put good intentions into the water of good health and strength and choosing to live. But the medicine and the Great Spirit had other plans.

It became that I had to prove I wanted to live and fight for my life; for as soon as I had finished the water, I began to purge. And I mean projectile vomit on the grass on my hands and knees. I had fasted all day, so this was a water and energetic vomit. This was my body's way to clear all the emotional trauma that this week had caused on my body (a lot of emotions and trauma are stored in our stomach and digestion, hence purging helps to clear and heal). This went on for hours and it was a battle of trying to drink water to hydrate, followed by immediate purge. I was becoming increasingly dehydrated.

I really thought I was going to die. My head and body were in so much pain and my brain felt like a raisin. In between purges I challenged myself to meditate and try to breathe. I connected with my mum and felt her intense grief for Kody and pain and sent her love and healing too, and for all my family. Then I would be interrupted by the need to purge again. When the purging finally ended, I felt emotionally and physically drained and still dehydrated. The challenge to fight for survival continued.

Eventually, exhausted, I lay down with some Palo Santo to cleanse and tried to integrate the learnings and the experience as the medicine subsided.

We closed the ceremony and went to have a watermelon. To our surprise the watermelon was bright yellow! This felt profound and had me questioning if we had entered a parallel universe where watermelons are yellow. It was funny and confusing. Turns out we did not change universes, but yellow watermelons actually pre-date red watermelons and are natural (and even more sweet!). Exhausted, we went to sleep (after I drank 2L of water). That night I woke up numerous times for a pee, my body still cleansing itself and clearing the pain and blockages. I had very broken sleep as a result.

When I woke up the next day I felt physically, mentally and emotionally drained, and still extremely dehydrated with a headache. I had lots of cayenne pepper and Celtic Sea salt in my lime water that morning. Although I felt rough, I felt different. I felt clear inside, no longer paralysed. I felt my emotionally body had pieced itself together again, still damaged and bruised, but in one piece.

I feel like now I must really live. I feel Kody with me. I feel grateful for my life again and to be alive, as I really think I was close to death through dehydration. I actually researched this and turns out, dehydration through Ayahuasca can be a cause of death! I had not been drinking enough the day of the ceremony (reduced self-care) and had been in the sweltering heat of 35+ degrees Celsius, adding to the dehydration I experienced.

I still feel sad, however I do not feel dead inside anymore. I feel comforted by Kody. I love Kody and set him free for his next adventure. As Tlilik Tekuani taught me, love is freedom. I am grateful to Kody for all the healing he brought me and all the valuable life lessons he taught me, and I celebrate his life and the blessing that we shared so much time and love together. He consistently helped me to find strength during my darkest nights.

Kody came into my life when I was 17 (I am now 27). Life for me at that time was dark and full of fear. My mind was warped at age 12 by horror movies watched at friends' houses. Most of my friends would be chatting but I became fixated on the images and sick story lines. I am a believer that anything is possible and therefore it shocked me to think that there are people out there who can even think up and imagine such horrible acts and ideas.

Interestingly, out of all of them, the worst film that impacted my mental health is only rated a 12 (although I disagree with this rating). It is called 'The lovely bones'. The basic storyline is a young teenage girl is stalked by her elderly neighbour who kidnapped her in the cornfield she walked through to get to school each day, and he took her into his underground lair in the field and did awful sick things. At this time, I was a young teenage girl, living in a village of predominantly old people and walking by myself through a field to get to school every day. This led to a solid belief within me that each day there was a very high chance of this happening to me and I would die. I said goodbye to my mum each morning as though it may be the last. This triggered great anxiety and depression which spanned all of my teenage years. I used to be terrified of our family home which is a solo farm house in the middle of the field. For years there were no curtains and at nighttime all the windows were black and I would imagine faces appearing and felt like I was being watched. There is a long drive through the field reaching the house and in winter it would be dark when I was walking home down this road. We were made to study 'The Woman in Black' in drama when I was 15, a horror story of a house down a long dark road. I then became terrified of evil spirits etc. In my mind I had a living hell.

As a result, I would go out partying and started drinking alcohol and taking drugs at age 13, a form of escapism I now see. I used to go to camping parties and spend time with my friends and people older than us. I loved rock music and going to gigs and raves, which was fun times, but often combined with alcohol or other things which were often given to me, I did not buy any. Easily influenced and enjoying new experiences and adrenaline in these settings was fun in the moment but not very healthy for my mind and body overall. I used to wear only black. I was diagnosed as severely clinically depressed and put on strong antidepressants at 15. As mentioned, these were increased to 60mg of Citalopram over time and I felt like a zombie. I had some bad experiences with men and other challenges and was lucky to receive much therapy in terms of counselling, CBT, Bowen and family support. It was an intense time indeed.

However, when Kody joined the family (we got him from the border collie rescue centre at age 1), my life changed. I loved him so much, love at first sight and I would take him for numerous nature walks a day (something I had not done as a previous hobby for myself).

This time with him exploring nature got me to view life in a new way. I was in awe at Mother Earth and seeing the beauty all around me so clearly. I saw how Kody was curious and happy all the time and he inspired me greatly. He took away my fears and I began to love where I lived, a place I previously hated due to the daily internal terror.

We would walk with the stars and I no longer felt afraid. He helped me to face the dark and realise that the darkness was less scary when I was in it and to embrace it rather than look at it through a window with a crazy imagination.

Kody saved me and kick started my healing journey, getting me on the right path and helped me to connect with my spirituality. My saviour, my best friend, my love and greatest teacher. My family. Soul connection forever.

***

I realise that now I must make him proud by "being more Kody"-present, happy, free, brave, fun and kind to everyone. Integrate all of his teachings from these ten years into each day. Time to live courageously, be spontaneous, say yes, take risks, really LIVE. Maybe I will go to China and train in the Kung fu Temples as I had thought to do after van life with Kody. We shall see where life's flow takes me.

So yeah that ceremony was the most intense experience of my life and the closest my soul has been to giving up. But I did not give up. I found my strength. And now? I feel unbreakable. I will bounce back from this. I know it and feel it.

The next day I did a cacao ceremony and cards, and I asked three questions. The first question was: 'What was the main learning to take from the ceremony?'. The card I pulled was 'Divine timing'. To me this is referring to my 'death day'... and the timing is not yet as I have much living and work left to do here. It also linked to Kody's departure

281

being divine timing, even though I do not feel it at this moment, but I must trust.

The second question I asked was "What is the main message for me from Kody?". The card I pulled was 'Spontaneity', about living life to the fullest, saying yes to adventures, having a courageous and out of the ordinary life. This matched exactly the message I felt from him during the ceremony so affirmed that super strong!

The final question I asked was "So what do I do now?" and the card I pulled was 'Worthiness' and discussed letting go of any feelings of guilt or shame, loving myself and feeling worthy and deserving of a great life. This felt very empowering and just the right thing to focus on as I am currently living day by day.

***

I am still at my friend's family home in Chiriqui (mainland Panama), where we did the ceremony, as they have been kind enough to allow me to stay. It has been great as the past couple of days I have been able to do my morning practices and self-care toolkit of meditation, workout, Qi Gong, Cacao, cards, fruit, sleep, stillness and family and friend communication. It is a safe haven for me at the moment. I am so grateful. We also went to a big waterfall the day after the ceremony, getting caught in a rainstorm in the jungle and jumping from a big rope swing, plunging into the cold deep water and feeling reborn. Nice.

I have been reflecting on this crazy intense fortnight and its process. There have been three people I have spent time with and shared my grief - three divine masculine men. Each supported me in different ways, which were needed at each stage of my process. Donatello was there in the initial shock and held me safe and helped me to feel alive and explored my pain with me so I did not feel alone. Then Harold held a ceremony for me which enabled my purging and clearing the toxic trauma, shock and emotional pain from my body and strengthened my spirit. Clearing my vessel. Then his brother, Hirim, inspired me with his positive words, insights and creativity, as to catapult me back to positivity and continue my soul mission. I am so grateful for each of these men holding space for me in the ways they did and in the order it happened. Universe, I trust you.

Which means I must trust that everything happens in divine timing, when it is supposed to. I must trust that Kody leaving the Earth at this time is how it is supposed to be. He lived happy and free and without pain and part of me feels he was given a choice about this and able to decide. In deciding to leave now, he did this to set me free, to allow me to really explore this world and go to all the places that call my soul. I feel like Kody wants to accompany me on these journeys and does not want me to feel restrained or attached. He wants to support me to fulfil my destiny. I love him so much. I must trust the process. My heart aches but I know I am strong and Kody is too. I feel him closer now than before and his energy is within me and around me. I send him so much love and freedom.

So, this brings us to the present moment as I am sitting here and leads to the question... What is next? I am still in the mode of self-care and healing. Living day by day.

I would like to spend more time travelling as I cannot face to go home right now. I would like to explore some more of Panama while I am here and then go to Guatemala, before returning to the UK. Once in the UK, who knows what I will do...

I am learning, if I get too set with any future plans, the universe likes the game of pulling the rug from under my feet, watching my world crumble and seeing how I rise up again. So I will say this is not a plan, just a "rough idea/ intention", and I will see what flows.

Universe, I trust you. **Now let's LIVE.**

54.   'Love is freedom' 09.03.2024

One of life's biggest learnings,
Is that love is freedom.

Sometimes when we love,
We can hold on too tight,
Scared to let go in case it might leave,
And leave it might.

This can cause many troubles, many pains...
Over time it can make us close down to love in this life game.

As when we become so attached to the things or ones we love,
We convince ourselves that without them,
Life takes a dark dip,
That we won't survive...

We give our well-being away to an external part,
disempowering our energy in the heart.
Then, if what we love goes,
in one way or another,
as often it does,
Our mental health plummets and hope can't get through

It shakes our world, we lose our way,

Life's meaning collapses, less stable, easily swayed.

Internal elements and structures crashing and tumbling,

Appetite gone, stomachs not rumbling,

We can't see a way through,

Where to turn or what is true…

Yet life can teach us what to do…

what I have learned let me share to you:

Love always starts from within our hearts,

use breath and intention to expand it.

Fill yourself up, to the brim of your cup,

Then overflow this love to the world, make it lit!

Still love others, connect and share our love that overflows,

We are here to connect deeply,

not stay in the shallows.

Finding the balance of deep connection without attachment,

is quite difficult,

but awareness and intention help bring this to action.

All are teachers when open to showing,

And be knowing,

That sharing love in this way is abundantly flowing,

Always enough to go around, pay it forward, keep going.

When loved ones pass over, we can still grieve…
But we can help them by letting go and sending love,
as that's what they need.

We want to allow their spirit to be expansive and free,
Not worrying about me,
Attached to us by our pain body…
They want to see us happy, thriving,
grateful the connection was ever made,
Not for too long huddled depressed at their grave.

Love is freedom, it needs no constraints,
Be blessed to have experienced such love and connection with
other souls and saints.
Celebrate their energy, love shared, lessons learned,
Have faith you will see them again, but don't yearn.

Relationships with others can feel sad too when they end,
So sad we may try and force them to mend.
Try to see your whole life path and how those lessons and
experiences helped your soul,
Together you may not grow old,
But the memories and transformations offered are gold,
And it was meant to happen that souls' cross paths with
purpose,
so I've been told.

Love is freedom.

Allow paths to divert,

Understand that each soul has a mission on this Earth.

You may be a deep part of that mission,

or you may be brief,

but love the fact you had the chance to meet.

Don't hold on too tight,

be present, don't fight,

And keep your self-love cup always filled within you.

Love is freedom,

love is acceptance,

love is the biggest blessing.

Non-attachment to future outcomes,

grateful for the past and present.

Loving fully each day, no condition.

Create it, believe it, that is your mission.

To really live is to live in love.

So, now let's REALLY live 💚 🐾

Following Panama, Donatello and I travelled to Guatemala, a destination I was determined to reach. We travelled all over, hiked and camped to witness an active volcano, visited the ancient Tikal temples- Mayan civilization in the jungle, experienced Semuc Champney- most beautiful waterfalls! A point could be made that I was determined to do as many things as possible to feel alive and deter the depression which was lurking.

We went to Lake Atitlan in Guatemala and did a workaway volunteer role for a few weeks. This involved walking 4 dogs up the mountain at sunrise daily, feeding them, caring for them. This was so nice as I wanted to connect with dogs to feel close to Kody. We also had air bNb responsibilities with bed making etc. I made a great friend with a Guatemalan lady called Rivka who was local to the area and she is just pure love!

I also met an amazing man for a fire ceremony, Buho Cruz, who holds fire ceremonies with offerings to the fire and calls in the 20 Nawals (Mayan spirit energies). Remarkably interesting. My Mayan energy is 10 Batz. This is like another version of 'star signs' from a different culture. Again, very relatable! They say different Mayan energies command different days, this is called the Mayan calendar. I am so grateful for all the amazing people I met on this travel.

A fun adventure I also had was meeting a creative friend who had a music studio in a nearby city. I met him at Lake Atitlan at a Mayan hip-hop fire ceremony and shared the 'self-care toolkit' poem with him when he asked if I was creative. He liked it and invited me to record it with him! A week later I caught 4 'chicken buses' to get to another city (not many tourists were there) and had fun recording a track and staying in his tree house! The next day he drove me back to the lake on his motorbike (approx. 2.5 hours) through the mountains. It was so crazy because it was crazy mist and we could barely see 1m in front of us, it was freezing and honestly pretty scary on these mad high and steep roads in the mountains with chicken buses flying around the corners!

For my flight back to UK from Guatemala I had to change planes at New York. I had to transfer to the other New York airport, so leave one, travel across the city to the other one! I made a friend when I was in Panama City for one night, who lives in New York, and he said he would take me on a 3-hour New York tour as I had 7 hours total between my first plane landing and second plane taking off. We had a wild 3 hours and saw so many classic New York things!

All New York bucket list things I saw. However, by the time I got to the second airport, check-in had closed by 10 minutes. I was still over an hour early for the flight, but no one could let me through. My bag was only hand luggage but as it was a cheaper airline there was no online check in to get my boarding pass. It was a rough moment as the staff were unhelpful and quite savage and told me I had to buy a new ticket for tomorrow. Another £350! As I ended up staying out there for 4 months, instead of 7 weeks, I went through alllll my life savings (spending what I was saving for the van for me and Kody). I only had a few hundred pounds left. I cried for a moment and then my friend found me and said "well then, just buy a ticket and let us enjoy your 24 hours in New York!" So, I brushed myself off and we had a wild time through the city of New York. So grateful for this friend.

I returned home end of April and all the grief for Kody was re-triggered. It was finally really real. This has been a crazy intense process. Lots of time by the old Oak where he is buried, playing him the flute, reading him poems, singing to him, meditating. I spent a lot of time there. Some songs I really connected to during this time were: 'Let you go- Deyaz', 'A Prayer of my own- Nick Mulvey', 'Mindfulness' and 'Heart Chakra by Mr Traumatik'.

I got back into work as needed to earn money as I was down to minimal funds. I was grateful to see family and friends and get back to Kung Fu and good routines.

***

The next poem I wrote reflecting on the war in Palestine and all the other wars and conflicts happening all over the world: Ukraine, the Congo, Yemen, Syria and every other place where there is unrest either internationally or civil wars.

55.   'Tears for the Earth and humanity'
08.06.2024

I shed tears for the Earth and humanity.

I feel the worlds suffering,

The pain of the collective energy.

The wars taking place around the world are pure monstrosities.

Shocked by the killings and humanity de-personalisation,

Feeling the current killers are a previous child trauma generation.

Those experiencing early trauma and receiving no love or support,

Leaves wounds open for indoctrination,

Propaganda, untruths, and hate can be taught.

Creating 'the enemy' by blowing differences out of proportion,

When actually, differences make life interesting,

and hold different wisdoms and fortunes.

Besides, we are basically the same!

We have similar body shapes and structures,

the same organs, emotions and belief in a Great Spirit oneness.

Maybe we call it different names...

But God, The Great Spirit, Allah, Yahweh, The divine,

All represent the same!

Different keys to unlock the same lock...

Let's together build bridges, remove all the blocks.

We must put a stop to those troubled souls in positions of power,

Unhealed are their minds, making killing decisions from up in their ivory tower.

Safe, protected, away from it all,

Sending their traumatised troops to bring and face the wrath of war and be subject to fall.

Most of whom are being exploited, blackmailed or brainwashed to join in.

Out of choice, many would prefer to be at home with family, eating and relaxing.

Conflicts are happening around the world for different reasons...

Some due to communities protesting for equality,

those in power call this 'treason'.

Some due to dictators being a dickhead every season.

Some due to different beliefs and religions,

Some due to land, resources, power, money,

Tactics to destroy and enslave are so cunning!

Some conflicts are just souls wanting MORE control,

as they are not satisfied or content with life,

So are trying to fill a never-ending hole.

This method they are using will never fill them with
contentment and love.

To do that they must be kind and spread this all around them,
below and above.

When will human beings see each other as siblings of the Earth
in this life?

Everyone is suffering and fighting fire with fire all sides.

Imagine if Aliens came to attack,

We would all come together,

the 'Earth Team inhabitants', and together rise.

Sending intentions of peace and balance every day.

I love you all my brothers and sisters of the Earth.

Regardless of your skin tone, language, cultures or beliefs,

I am always here for you, as we are one,

you and me.

Summer 2024: I have been working across the country to complete holistic occupational therapy assessments for children and teenagers in residential homes and specialist schools and this interesting and fulfilling. They love my toolkit for the assessment which includes nerf gun (hand eye coordination), Boxing pads (strength, balance, coordination, emotional regulation, breathing), weighted blanket and singing bowls (Relaxation, emotional and sensory regulation), animal oracle cards, magic tricks and necklace warrior healer necklace making (fine motor skills, understanding instructions) and all my sensory toys and fidgets.

I went to a drum and bass Mr Traumatik rave with a friend. I love drum and bass and do not need to take anything to get hyped. It felt great to be sober and drove home arriving with the sunrise. Not to mention was in the last 5 people still dancing at the end(!).

I was invited on a road trip with Tlilik Tekuani, in June. This included going to Stone Henge for Summer Solstice and going to Glastonbury festival! This was a free crew ticket, and I am so grateful.

At Glastonbury, I ended up performing at a fire playing the big drum stood on a rock with feathers in my hair and face paint for Tlilik Tekuani's Mexican fire ritual, with a couple of hundred people watching(!).

This was last minute and without a rehearsal! I played the drumkit often from age 9-15 so I had some drumming experience, but no recent practice and my forearms were burning! Before the performance, I asked Tlilik Tekuani what to do with my face; I am usually overly expressive with my facial expressions and perhaps a bit goofy at times. He told me it was a ritual so I need to be serious. This can be a challenge for me, but he told me to connect with the big fire and stare at it, so that is what I did.

During the ritual, he also handed me fire on a stick, a new experience for me (no practice), in front of this crowd. I waved it around a bit and then for some reason felt the best option I could do was to stand like a serious statue of liberty hahaha. It was so out of my comfort zone but such a great and transformational experience. Face the fear and do it anyway. Live full, just like Kody.

Afterwards children were talking to us and one of them asked me if I am Mexican too. This melted me and I am pleased that perhaps my performance was convincing… either way I am choosing to take this as a complement ;).

***

At this festival, to my surprise, I saw the man previously mentioned in my 'express girl' poem. It triggered a lot of anxiety and strange feelings within me. Weirdly, when he saw me in the crowd, he waved... this surprised me and I was like what (?!). It was then that I realised he had no idea the deep impact his action had on me... he wanted to meet and I was unsure… but after thinking about it, decided perhaps this clarity was needed and I needed to make peace as I cannot be feeling anxious every time, I think I see him. I do not want to be triggered. I am strong and healed now.

We met on the last day. I said we need to talk serious, he said he knew. I expressed everything. He listened. I told him the impact it had and how it was unacceptable what happened.

He apologised and agreed he messed up. I told him I wrote a poem, and he asked me to share it. I warned him that I am angry towards him in it. He said it was okay and listened to a recording of my poem I had. He took it all in. He then genuinely apologised from the bottom of his heart. He was actually so kind and open and listened fully, denied nothing. He said he is so sorry and never intended to damage me as I have a beautiful heart. He said this he has learned a lot from and will take this lesson forward and be mindful not to misread situations or make assumptions. I hope this whole experience makes him never do such an action again.

I feel a weight has been lifted and that has been the last bit of my healing. I know for many people this closure is not possible for a variety of reasons, so I am grateful that this happened for me. He supported the idea of me sharing the poem in this book.

***

Following Glastonbury, I was invited to my good friends sacred wedding ceremony abroad. They booked and paid for everything for me, which blew me away, and I am so grateful for these beautiful souls, so blessed to share time with them in this life.

This ceremony I met with Grandmother Ayahuasca once again. Another profound experience. The night before, we watched a movie and it included a dog (cartoon). This triggered me somehow and I went out in the woodland mountain and cried and whaled and allowed myself to crumble once again into all-consuming grief. I stayed there over an hour in the dark, releasing it all. When finished, I did a smoke cleanse and a prayer to Kody.

During the medicine ceremony the next day, I connected with Kody and Jim and Grandad so deeply within my heart, seeing their faces clearly in my heart centre, their love giving me strength in this life, not weakness.

Since then, my grief has felt different. My heart is no longer broken, but full and radiant. Sad of course, I miss them all greatly, especially my Kody boy. But I have him with me now wherever I am, to guide my heart and my spirit to be joyful and free.

56.   'Family' 13.07.2024

I am so grateful, I feel so blessed,
I am too blessed to be stressed,
I am so content; I don't need more or less.
My heart feels strong, held, loved, caressed,
My spirit feels calm, peaceful, chilled, at rest.
My body feels healthy, strong, clean vessel, my best.

I feel more connected than ever to my family,
This term describing my ancestors, blood connections,
those who are close with me.
As I grow older, this family is expanding,
Through shared groups, experiences and interests,
having our life paths crossing and meandering.
Connecting with hearts from all walks of life,
Providing many gifts and many insights,
Supporting my spirit to shine super bright.

I thank you my mother, Dear Tracy,
You are an apple of my eye,
You are a super mum, a super human oh my,
You hold me so safe, you inspire me greatly,

With you I speak my mind,
you believe in me intensely,
always listen intently.
You are so sweet, so pure,
so innocent, your spirit I adore.

Every bone, cell and part of your being is benevolent,
You are a great teacher and my closest friend,
I love you in this life and far beyond its end.

Thankyou my mother,
my birth mother and all the others,
All the others who have treated me with feminine caring energy,
Presenting in various forms, looking after me.

And of course, the mother of all, dear Mother Earth,
Nurturing, caring, providing for us all,
This magnificent home and providing us tasty fuel! (like mangos)
And for all the medicines we need to self-heal,
And to help us expand our mind and spirit field.

Thank you to my grandmother's,
wisdom carriers, rays of sunshine and light,
Always open to connect, no judgements or stress,
You make everything feel alright.

Thank you to Grandmother Aya,

Your spirit and insight have lifted me higher,

Transformation of pain to strength,

Kody now strong in my heart, your method I admire.

My recent meeting with you, beautiful medicine,

has left me inspired.

I love you my father, super cool and loving Dad,

With you I have had fun adventures,

a listening ear and many laughs to which I'm glad.

You are understanding, you care,

you are considerate, funny and fair,

I am so grateful for the connection we share.

I love and thank all protective father energy,

Gifted to me by my stepdad, family members and good friends, there's many.

I feel protected and guided,

Divine masculine's are plenty.

And oh, Father Sky, watching over and protecting all,

Your skies of sunsets, rainbows and stars

are such an awesome miracle.

To my Grandad, Oak spirit, up there in the sky,

Your inspiration is with me every day in this life,

I feel your presence and still connect with your spirit strongly,

You helped the veil between worlds to be thinner,

Connecting me more with my spirituality.

To my Grampa here on Earth,
Blessings to you my dear friend,
good times and deep chats had a plenty,
sharing perspectives, insights we blend.

Grandfather spirit of the Otac toad of the tobacco,
Your protection and healing ceremonies,
Have helped my troubles melt away like snow,
with joy to show!
Grateful to have met and connected with your spirits energies,
The wisdom shared now known,
my mind has been greatly blown,
New understandings of this reality.

All my sisters and brothers,
Of those I have many,
Within my birth family
And all new friends and souls I meet.
We are all children of Mother Earth and Father sky,
Walking the path of life together, carried by our feet.

Grandmother moon, Grandfather sun,
Uncle mountain, Auntie Ocean, cloud Son.
Recently I discovered that I come from the star Andromeda,
But I learned that I am able to also belong and feel at home
here.

The trees, the animals and flowers, my beautiful family,

The one we all belong,

You, you,

You

and them

and us

and me.

I want to acknowledge the importance of understanding generational trauma. I feel immense gratitude for my family and the positive aspects they bring, I also recognise that each member has their own journey, shaped by past experiences and struggles. The pain and patterns we encounter can often be inherited from those who came before us. As we navigate our own paths, I encourage you to love harder, forgive more, and lead by example.

By breaking these cycles and consciously addressing our experiences, we can heal not only ourselves but also our families. Remember, acknowledging and understanding family members experiences and generational pain can empower us to transform our narratives and create a more compassionate future and connect with family without judgement but with acceptance and understanding.

***

57.   'I choose Joy' 03.08.2024

I have a choice everyday
And I choose Joy!
Positive thoughts to start my morning,
As negative thoughts destroy.
I choose to plant seeds for thought flowers to bloom,
To brighten my life perspective,
Less doom and gloom.

I intend for my mind to be positive and kind,
I intend to light up the room and shine!
I intend to be kind and non-judgemental to all that I meet,
To see the bigger picture and the lessons of each person I
observe or greet.

I allow myself to feel intense emotions as they come,
I honour them, feel their depths, accept them,
But not allow them to, with me, become one.
This is not about 'false positivity',
We all can feel angry, anxious or sad,
an essential part of life it seems.

The world offers a vast sea of negativity,

But like a ship, I cannot be sunk,

if I do not allow it to leak inside of me.

I am not helping world situations by feeling outraged,
depressed, fearful...

This adds more bad energy to the mix,

Feeding beings who are fuelled by energy like this.

Of course, I can feel this way,

triggered by world happenings I feel helpless to change.

But a way I have found to connect,

with these happenings, not to block or reject,

is to get my energy positive and centred,

then meditate and pray,

sending love and peace to all those intended.

This impacts the balance

of dark and light energy,

I feel sending light where there is dark,

Is a way to help influence from a far, you see.

I want it all to stop,

I want all to be free,

I want the humans of the Earth to unite as one,

to live in harmony.

So I intend this, imagine this,

as what life on Earth could be.

Manifestation of thoughts and feelings is strong,

Many people holding this intention can physically manifest our planets destiny.

Consistency is key,

Slip it into your morning routine,

Once you begin, it will fit right in, you'll see.

Tune into gratitude first and last thing,

Begin and end our day, focusing on our blessings.

Thank you for this safe space that I sleep,

Thank you that I am alive today, to this day greet.

Thank you for all the drinks and the food that I eat,

Thank you for my health, my current abilities that are in reach.

Don't focus on what's wrong, focus on what's right,

You may not right now be physically able,

but maybe you have sight.

You may have an illness, disease, infection,

But you may have the ability to read and to write.

You may be really sick or really broken,

But focus on your breath,

Connect with music,

Your mind is still open.

There is truth that our mind and focus impact our health,

People have healed the 'unhealable', walked again,

shocking doctors who do not have this intervention on their theory shelf.

So much is possible, but our minds we must train to be strong,

Focus on the good and what you can be grateful for,

don't focus on what is lacking or wrong.

This impacts our energy by lifting our mood,

This uplifted energy is when more healing takes place

For our highest good.

Visualise self in good health, imagine and intend what could…

Affirmations daily in the mirror are so powerful…

Rewiring our brain, new self-beliefs understood.

At the very least, it will make you feel more positively good.

Gratitude for Earth and Sky,

Beautiful planet so much light!

Gratitude that my soul chose to come here, to live the challenge
of life.

Gratitude that the greater the Earth challenge, the more faith
God has in you,

To find new levels of inner strength,

helping soul and spirit to expand, I feel is true.

So I choose joy, no matter what life throws my way,

Life events are sure to be more challenging on some days,

And that's okay,

I will with the hurricane sway,

And then return to my centre

to tune back in to my joy at being alive today.

58.   'Sisterhood' 18.08.2024

This poem I wrote reflecting on all the amazing women I have crossed paths with, supported and been supported by.

Love to all my home girls,

My witches,

My sisters.

Love to my female companions,

Friends, family

And acquaintances.

I support you,

Wonderful women,

Fantastic females,

Lovely ladies.

I support you gorgeous girls, wild witches,

Fair maidens, wise crones,

and of course,

all mothers to all babies.

I want you to flourish,

I want you to shine,

I want you to express your true self and be connected with the divine.

I want to see you radiate and glow,
I want all your dreams to come true.

I want you to feel backed by your sisters on this Earth,
feeling supporting through and through.

I want all your hopes and wishes to become reality.
I want you to live in love, surrounded by good company.
I want you to be safe,
And I want you to live free.
I want you to be empowered by yourself internally.

I want you to believe in you, as I do,
I want you to shine your light bright and true,
I want you to look in the mirror and be in pure love
with the very special beautiful you.

I pray each day brings you more love, more joy,
more wisdom, more clarity.
I pray that you trust your intuition,
your love and your sanity.
I pray that women support and rejoice each other,
Coming together to heal and support humanity.

***

I have been feeling my appreciation for my job and my practice as an Occupational Therapist. As mentioned throughout this book, Occupational Therapy can be applied to everyone, as we are all aiming for balance between our self-care, productivity, and leisure occupations, striving for occupational balance, which increases quality of life, health, wellbeing, and fulfilment.

I am so grateful that I am in a position where I am able to support others and make a difference, big or small. I have worked in the community, supporting people in their homes to be more independent by introducing aids or housing adaptations and teaching skills. I have worked in acute men's mental health rehabilitation hospital which was very intense but so rewarding. I have worked in Autism diagnosis and sensory intervention for adults and children. I have worked across the UK to deliver holistic occupational therapy assessments to children in foster care, residential homes and specialist schools, to identify need and then train the staff and family around the child what interventions to introduce into daily life.

Now I am working with a city school for children who have social and emotional difficulties, many of whom have experienced shocking abuse or trauma, or may be involved with gangs and the dreaded 'zombie knife'. I also work with a school for children with severe/ complex learning difficulties and Autism, most of whom are non-verbal and face many challenges. It is a diverse client group, and every child is uniquely different. I am learning and problem solving on my feet, and it is challenging but I am grateful that I am able to support them in the ways that I can.

There are not enough Occupational Therapists to meet current societal needs. If you like to help people, problem solve, think creatively and enjoy the holistic approach, I encourage you to explore the career of Occupational Therapy. The world needs your love, care and ideas!

59.   'Occupational Therapy' 24.09.2024

Occupational therapy,

Is a perfect job role for me,

Supporting people to bring positivity,

Reaching their goals, making progress on the daily.

Solving the problems we can see,

removing barriers that are blocks to daily living,

Teaching skills, helpful aids, and interventions we are giving.

To empower the individual adult or child,

in prisons, schools, hospitals,

Some settings can be wild!

Person centred holistic care is our approach,

We are just here to guide and empower,

To teach, support and coach.

The person leading the therapy, is the individual in question,

They are the boss I must mention.

What is meaningful to them? What brings them joy?

What causes tension?

What are their goals and dreams for their lifetime in this
dimension?

I am not here to judge decisions, or tell people what to do,

I will share information,

then your decision I will support you through.

As OT's we like to think outside the box,

New ideas and techniques, to unlock the box lock.

Nothing is impossible, we see with a lens of positive possibility.

We teach the importance of occupational balance,

between self-care, leisure and productivity.

Everything we do as humans, comes into these three categories,

Important to balance work and play

and have time for sleep.

If we are not productive, we can struggle to make ends meet,

We may live in a mess, with no food to eat.

If we do not do self-care like wash, relax, exercise and sleep,

Our physical body will shut down, unable to function or leap.

If we do not engage in leisure,

Our life zest decreases in measure,

Our joy and meaning for life lost,

a now hidden pirate's treasure.

All are equally important, not one or the other,

To be in balanced in your occupations,

Offers fulfilment to feel again and discover,

Good quality of life increased and uncovered.

If the challenges are many, break them down into bits.

Problem solve each one, finding the root cause of it.

Then think outside the box for a solution,

Trust me there may likely be more than one!

Teach skills, try aids and work always on self-love.

Get creative in your ideas,

Embrace the joy when a set goal is achieved,

And when successfully decreasing any fears.

Occupational Therapy can be applied to everyone,

We are all human beings who need to function.

If you like solving problems and helping people,

then this profession calls to you,

To join the Occupational Therapist community,

In high demand but we are few...

this planet needs you

This summer I attended a spiritual, healing festival, for the 5th year in a row. The year I began writing 2020, to now, 2024. It is not running next year, taking a break. This marks the end of the cycle. This festival has been transformational each year. This year my highlights included meeting the Zen Samuri from Japan who inspired me with his energy and peace when I attended his calligraphy and samurai sword training class! This practice is not just about using a sword; it is about controlling inner energy and emotions, remaining present and using the breath. (hence the Zen). I feel very drawn to expand my insight and skills in Chinese and Japanese martial arts. He invited me to train with him at his school on Samurai island in Japan…

At the festival, practicing pray mantis shaolin kung fu was also a highlight, in addition to a vibey Kirtan and having the best girls camp, where I connected deeply with beautiful magical women, a real sisterhood.

Now, my focus turns to three main things.

One is working with specialist schools to deliver occupational therapy to children and teens with complex mental, physical, emotional, and social needs.

The other, to bring Balanced Flame Qi Gong online, extending this self-healing tool globally, honouring Jim's legacy.

The third, to live a life of adventure and new experiences, which keeps my zest for life high, allowing me to be the best occupational therapist, friend, and family member I can be.

And maybe go to China and Japan to train Kung Fu, Chinese healing techniques and the Samurai. Who knows…

60.   'Qi Gong' 06.09.2024

I have touched on this briefly,
But let's take a moment to go in more deeply.

"Guiding the flow of energy,
Under the cloak of invisibility,
To organs, emotions, spirit,
Brings tranquillity,
This is a tool in our toolkit see." (self-care toolkit poem)

The ancient Chinese practice of Qi Gong,
Needs to be shared as a mainstream healthcare intervention.
It works best in prevention,
So start today and teach kids from day one.
It can aid all kinds of situation.
To improve your health takes daily practice and dedication.
Dedication to keep energy flowing, no stagnation.
Unblock our channels so our energy flows,
To all of the places it needs to go,
Feel grounded, breathe deep,
Focus on intention keep,
Engage with your body from head to feet.

Connect with each organ,

Smile into it,

Connect with the element and attributes associated with it,

Stay focused, don't quit.

Follow the creative cycle,

The route energy flows through organs to complement our health.

Do this inner alchemy Qi Gong practice,

And reap the wellness wealth.

Heart is fire, glowing red light,

That's where we start.

Our love, joy, compassion,

our unique passionate spark!

Lighting our way through even the darkest dark.

Ashes from the fire, fertilise the Earth,

Fertilised nourished Earth, increases nutrients surplus!

Our stomach, pancreas and spleen,

On our left side of our torso,

imagine them with shining yellow light, healthy and clean.

Our openness, fairness and trust,

These traits help our perspective adjust.

The Earth holds the metal of the lungs-
Attributes of courage and assertiveness,
Increasing our effectiveness.
With lungs expansive and strong,
We stand tall, we stand proud,
We stand up to what's wrong.

The metal attracts the water to the kidneys,
Be sure to keep them hydrated please!
They like to be warm,
And have fresh clean water,
Then they function as they 'ought ta
So if they are cold, warm them up,
Hot tea from a cup.
When in balance they help us to be soothed, gentle and calm,
Nervous system is peaceful,
Good sleep, no need to be alarmed.

The wonderful water feeds the wood of the liver,
Strong sturdy liver,
helping us to deliver,
toxins to the river,
Out of our body so diseases don't linger.
When in balance, liver brings us kindness and generosity,
Not to mention uplifted positivity.

This strong wood completing the cycle,
fuelling the fire in our heart,
the place from which we did start.

There's a brief example of 'inner alchemy Qi Gong'
Explore it further for more insights to be won ('Master Mantak Chia').

Qi Gong trains us to develop our sense of energy,
To feel and move something we can't normally see,
You will be able to read life situations with more ease,
More tuned in and intuitive.

You can learn to cultivate and direct energy around your body,
To different organs, limbs, intentions,
Or sending healing energy to somebody.

You will learn to feel energy with your hands,
and move it at will,
At this point you have unlocked an epic healing skill.

To develop this sense, comes with persistence and time,
Easier for those already sensitive and intuitively inclined.
Trust in your experience and hold the intention of healing,
Even without noticing the feeling,
you're doing wonders for your health and well-being.

Explore this practice for yourself,

feel empowered,

You can impact your health and wellbeing,

in life force energy showered.

There are many different styles and practices of Qi Gong:

Inner, outer, healing techniques and Qi Gong massage can be done.

Especially for children, this massage benefits,

Clearing toxins from their systems,

Our lifestyle gives many toxic hits.

We as adults and parents can to them make a difference,

Through a 15-minute daily massage to regulate their senses,

To clear blocks and bring yang down so they are no longer restless,

To allow yin to flow up,

Nourishing and effortless.

Heal yourself and build your energy.

Then share to others,

This healing tool you have explored

and discovered.

It's hard to truly explain this to another,

It is through their own experience,

that the mystery they will uncover.

Life, let's go

The initial poem surfaced at 23; now, 28, I am reflecting on this transformative journey and my ideas and experiences expressed through poetry. While uncertain of the future, I trust in a divine unfolding of my life path, guided and protected.

I set my intention for a life of love, fulfilment, and adventure, spreading light to uplift others in their darkness, and welcoming others light which supports me during my times of darkness too. An intention to grow in strength through the challenges and live the fullest life experience I can, in Kody's honour.

To "be more Kody", joyful, present, loving and free. Replacing any fear with curiosity... and just go for it, take the risk, take a chance, dream, hope, pray, love without limits. I feel his spirit will join in for many of my adventures yet to come, as well as having his own new adventures on the other side, where I will be reunited with him again one day.

There is a light within death which is in meeting all the loved ones gone before us. But until my time comes, I will live each day in this life with gratitude, compassion, generosity and joy in my heart, making each day sacred, marvelling at the wonder of everything. This beautiful planet Earth, within this solar system, extending further out with stars, planets and other galaxies. Too big to comprehend. Such an intricate creation. Wow.

***

The last poem is a final thought to leave you with. It is a reminder of our magnificence and prompts us to feel connected with the oneness of everything. This was written for my dear cousin Emma in the lead up to her passing from this Earth dimension and into the next. When people are soon to leave this life, conversations, and acknowledgment of what may happen next can be welcomed and approached with curiosity, which can help to decrease fear of the unknown which is too often, unspoken.

It is a certainty that the day will come for each of us to leave this Earth plane and pass over... life and death are intertwined and co-exist, so it is healthy and balanced to give death equal respect, curiosity, and consideration to help prepare us for this day.

A reminder that we are currently on Earth living through a physical body, but this is just one chapter of our soul's journey.

61.'Crystals and Stars' 13.02.2023

We are made of Earth and Sky,
We contain crystals and stars.

Balanced above and below,
Golden light in our centre does show,
All are a magnificent work of art.

We contain trees and sunshine,
Flowers, and light
We really are able to shine super bright.

We are rocks, we are rain,
We are sea and we are caves,
We are rainbows, we are lakes,
We are birds and we are snakes,
We are all animals that have been on Earth to this day!

We are thunder, we are lightning,
We can be so damn striking,
We are sunsets, we are sunrises,
Yes we are so delighting!

We are rivers, we are sand,
We are clouds – and
We can be a silver lining in this world - yes we can!

We are Earth, Fire, Water and Air,
We are space, energy, metal, light,
And we can have a heart that cares

Cares and connects to all that we are,
Our energetic roots holding crystals at the Earth's core,
Our light beam reaching up to the farthest star-
Connected so wide and far!

Yet it is also what we hold within us-
in this life concentrated,
but in the next life we expand into EVERYTHING- Trust!

Death is not The End,
it is simply to transform and transcend,
back to the source from which we did descend.

A return home, embraced in love,
We are everything once more,
Still able to guide and protect loved ones
Who are still in human form.

That's why we feel those who have passed over,
In the sunsets, oak trees, bluebells and clovers.
The Robin which sits on the window
And the twinkling stars guiding us where to go.

When we transform, we can choose to become guardian angels,
Leaving feathers and signs for family and friends we are able.

We are still here just no longer in a concentrated form,
We are expansive as our spirit has transformed.
Just as a Crystal and a Star are concentrations of Earth and Sky,
That is the same as how we have lived this current life.

Enjoy this present moment,
Be yourself, play your part.
And always remember,
We are all made of
Crystals
and
Stars.

Thankyou

Well thank you for joining me on these insights into my journey. My wish is that it may have inspired you, made you feel you are not alone or maybe you have found some of it insightful, relatable or perhaps just amusing or interesting.

I continue sending you love and joy, a big hug and extra ignition to your beautiful golden light in your heart to expand around your whole being. Never forget your connection to the divine, your ability to access this and your own personal power and wisdom.

Be true to you, trust your gut and speak your truth.

Truth is love.

No masks, no judgements, just your energy which is what makes you:

The Beautiful You.

Enjoy the adventure, have lots of fun and joy, embrace it all.

Make this life one to remember.

Know that you deserve love in its highest forms, from the world and from within.

Much love from my heart to your heart,

AHO.

My Gratitude in writing

I want to express my gratitude in writing to so many!

I thank all of my family and friends, especially my close ones, my mum, my dad, my Special and wise Granny June, my sister. My stepdad, my stepmum, my Nana, Grampa, stepbrothers, amazing friends and those who I have 'just clicked' with. Those who have supported me through thick and thin, through the good the bad and the ugly. Through the wacky and unbelievable. Through the intense and the magic.

So much love for all the supportive women and sisters in my life, this moon tribe is forever expanding and growing. Supporting and loving one another unconditionally.

Thank you to each and every person who has come onto my path as all the acts of kindness, conversations, experiences and lessons have shaped me and helped me to grow and transform.

I am grateful to Jim and to have shared a powerful, profound connection and for the teachings he shared to me. I am grateful for all these gifts he left me with and all he opened my eyes too. I am so grateful to have had the honour of meeting him, receiving healing from him and learning such magic, knowledge and wisdom. I am grateful for his continued love and support in spirit, his appearance in dreams and continued guidance.

I am so grateful to Mother Earth and Father Sky who inspire me daily, who ground us, uplift us and share their abundance of love and healing energy. I am grateful to all our angels, guides and ancestors who support us, guide us, protect us and hold us and who always answer our prayers. Thank you. I am so grateful to The Great Spirit and beyond, for this life experience I am living… I am grateful for this adventurous rollercoaster and opportunity to learn and grow and expand my consciousness. Thankyou life!

And of course, I am so grateful for Kody, the beautiful Border collie dog in my life. He has been with me throughout the crazy last 10 years, by my side as I ride all the waves, all the intense emotions and all the healing I have gone through. He remains positive and present and loves me unconditionally. He has been present with me when I write my poems and heal in the woods, and he has always kept me feeling a state of love as the love I have for him is out of this world. My angel, my baby, my best friend. Thank you.

(This I wrote before the book had completed, as I kept adding poems above). I now thank Kody's spirit who is still by my side, and I, by his.

Lastly, I am grateful to me.

I am grateful I have never given up on myself. I am grateful for my strength, my courage and my humour to help guide myself through any darkness.

I am grateful for my playfulness and my love of adventure. I am grateful for my presence through every experience, every sensation, every thought and every emotion. Thank you.

And thank you, wonderful reader, for your openness and curiosity and for the being that you are.

The Beautiful You.

Much love.

AHO.

Part 2/ Appendix

SELF-CARE TOOLKIT

I decided to collate some of the things that are in my self-care toolkit, mentioned throughout this book, as a reference guide. These are things I have tried and explored and found super beneficial! From here, you may choose to explore some of these which resonate with you and this may lead you to add them to your own self-care toolkit.

Remember to tune into your own body, do your research, and consult with local facilitators and experts if you decide to explore these areas. I am sharing these experiences because they have helped me, and my understanding is that everyone is unique, so different things work for different people. I am experienced in some things mentioned and novice in others. I enjoy exploring health and wellbeing practices from all around the world and different cultures and I feel there are many more tools to discover and add to my self-care toolkit as I go through this life, exciting!

Contents: Self-Care Toolkit ideas

1. Meditation
(Mindfulness meditation and visualisation meditation)

This was a huge transformational pivot point for me and really started my spiritual exploration. I had done some during my teens at my auntie's yoga class, however I started a consistent daily mindfulness meditation practice when I joined a weekly mindfulness meditation in the city I lived in at the time (age 19). Mindfulness Meditation is about allowing the mind to clear, focusing on all which is present, such as the breath, sounds and body sensations. It is helpful to have a guide talk you through how to do this as you practice or on the days when concentration sees more challenging.

My teacher has some great examples of this. These can be found through www.Symran.co.uk under 'audio guidance'. His technique and teaching set me up to guide myself, embodying what he taught me. Do this for ten minutes morning and night and life can be transformed. Doing this for two weeks, my years of anxiety and depression melted away and I saw the world with eyes of awe and beauty and gratitude. Letting go of the past and future, which can take up so much head space!

An app I have used which offers a variety of meditations, talks and poems is called 'Insight timer'. A lady on there who talks through gentle and soothing techniques is called 'Sarah Blondin' and she makes me feel as though I am on a cloud every time. My favourite is 'Life as a Sacred Art'.

There may be local meditation groups or sessions in your area and for sure in the cities. Search via social media tags and accounts to see what could align for you. The power of meditation as a group is impressive and I did my university dissertation for final year on this topic, after I was so amazed by my own experience of this.

2. Morning and Evening Breathing

A quick, easy and effective practice is to complete three deep breaths into the belly (lower dantian) area. Breathe in through the nose and out the mouth, expanding the belly on the in breath, drawing upon Earth and Sky energies.

Hold the intention of recalling and gathering your energy in your belly area, which is called your lower dantian and is your main energy centre. To do this in the morning and night is a great technique to start and end the day feeling centred, recalling and gathering your energy. Try to build it into daily routine in bed when you wake up and when you're about to sleep.

3. Deep Breaths

To support emotional regulation utilise breathing techniques, breathing in through the nose and using the out breath through the mouth to release and let go of anger, anxiety, tension or stress from the body.

It is beneficial to do numerous times throughout the day. Leave sticky note reminders around your house, in your car: "Breathe".

The breath is a powerful tool we have to regulate our emotions and cleanse our system. I would suggest looking into 'Breathwork' workshops or video guidance. For example: "Wim Hof Method Guided Breathing for Beginners (3 Rounds Slow Pace)" on YouTube (see below).

4. Breathwork

This is where you do consecutive deep breaths in through the nose and out the mouth, as large circular breaths, for a minimum of 30 breaths, and then breath out and hold the breath, not breathing in. See how long you can remain in that stillness and noticing the impact and feelings in the body. When you can hold the breath no longer, take a deep breath in through the nose and hold for 15-20 seconds, before releasing out the mouth and returning breathing to normal. This is often done for 3 rounds but can be done more, especially during guided group practice. Again, it trains our bodies to increase stress tolerance, in addition to helping lower resting heartbeat and numerous other health benefits. I encourage exploration of this practice and guidance on Wim Hof's website. Furthermore, it can be powerful and supportive to practice this in a group breathwork workshop session which you will likely find in your local city or even online sessions.

5. Qi Gong

Qi Gong is a healing martial art that dates back 5000 years and originated in China. Qi Gong means "working with energy, developing vitality, or cultivating life". It involves working with Qi (universal life force energy) to heal, balance and enhance the body and all its organs, the mind, the emotions, and the spirit. So simply, it is working with energy.

Qi Gong is a fusion of three essential elements: breath, movement, and intention. Qi, the universal life force, is the key to unlocking our spiritual potential and enhancing our sense of energy. We are familiar with our primary senses of sight, sound, touch etc but some of us are less practiced in using our sense of energy. We all have this sense and Qi Gong is one way to develop our sensitivity to it, which then unlocks further potential.

Many people have come across Tai Chi, which is from the same philosophy as Qi Gong and shares similarities. The difference is that Qi Gong often uses more basic movements, which I personally prefer, as I feel this makes it more accessible to people and can be easier to learn.

Qi Gong complements Kung Fu, the hard, warrior-like martial art. The balance between these two forms of martial arts is the yin-yang principle, the balance between the warrior and the healer. There are numerous online videos, in person group classes and retreats where you can learn Qi Gong. I am working to share and record the style of Qi Gong that Jim taught me.

6. Bamboo Sticks

The Qi Gong stick, composed of multiple slender bamboo sticks, is strategically applied to specific areas of the body—organs, meridians (energy lines), limbs, bones, and joints.

I was introduced to Qi Gong sticks by Jim in 2018. In 2022, I furthered my training at Tao Garden in Thailand, immersing myself in the practice of inner alchemy Qi Gong with Master Mantak Chia for an entire month. Each morning, the use of Qi Gong sticks served as a powerful reminder of their remarkable health benefits.

Master Chia explains that the bamboo sticks create vibrations that help open the pores in our bones. This is great for strengthening bones. The vibrations also shake out toxins from our muscles, organs, and fasciae, and break down deposits of uric acid while relieving tension in the body. Using the Qi Gong sticks can also encourage the growth of new stem cells, boost circulation, and help the lymphatic system clear out toxins (like mentioned with Qi Gong massage), especially breaking down blockages. It is a way to clear energy pathways so our energy can move freely throughout our body.

In addition to all these health benefits, using the Qi Gong sticks are a fantastic way to wake up, connect with our body, and feel alive and present. Just remember to be gentle and not hit too hard. If you do not have a Qi Gong stick, you can use your cupped hands and pat the energy down and out your body through hands and feet. This helps to clear the lymphatic system, remove blocks, increase circulation and feel embodied! Especially focus on key areas prone to toxin build up, such as the armpits and behind the knees.

If you are interested to follow a routine for using a Qi Gong stick you can go to this Website to access the free short course video: www.balancedflame.co.uk

7. Kung Fu/ Martial arts/ Exercise/ Yoga

Exercise is so good in general, releasing endorphins and helping us to feel happy and our bodies healthy, strong, and fluid. Any exercise is good- walk, run, swim, yoga etc. I try to input 15–30-minute workout and yoga routine at the beginning of my day and I feel more awake, more energised, and nicely stretched for my day! (Not achieved everyday mind- because life!). Stretching and opening the body at least a few times a week is so important as we often spend numerous hours either sat at a desk, slouching in a chair, standing, lying down or making repetitive physical movements. Some shapes we rarely make with our body and as a result we become stiff and lose our full range of movement over time and our posture may become hunched over and tight.

Martial arts are great in so many ways. Teaching strength, flexibility, self-discipline, respect, focus and emotional regulation. I like Kung Fu as it balances the Qi Gong I practice, Yin Yang balance, supporting us to be the warrior and the healer- but any martial art is good.

I have been using boxing pads in my therapy sessions with children and teens who have difficulty regulating their emotions and it has been very effective in helping emotional outlet and channelling intense feelings, releasing them in a constructive and safe way. This, followed by calming deep pressure activities such as wrapping in a weighted blanket and listening to relaxing sound, such as singing bowls, can be great to regulate the emotions and can be done as part of the daily routine. The sensory feedback from this is helpful in many ways.

8. Shakti Mat: Acupressure

This is a spikey mat which can be laid on (bare back) on the bed. It gives acupressure and although initially uncomfortable in the first few minutes, it leads onto deep muscle relaxation and supports in feeling relaxed for sleep. My friends brought me this for a birthday a few years ago and I use it most nights! Google Search 'Shakti mat' or 'Acupressure mat' for more information.

9. The Body Scan: To relax the body and for sleep

Feel the sensations in the body and use the breath to breathe into each body part to support its relaxation using the outbreath to relax the muscle. Scan from the head, down the body towards the feet. Always go this way as this helps calm the body for sleep- scanning feet to head is more awakening so could be done in morning routine. Search online for guided body scans which can offer audio guidance if unsure on how to guide yourself. It can take as little as 1-2 minutes.

10. Nature and Sky Gazing

Time in nature every day. Look around at the plants, the trees, the sky. Feel connected to this magnificent world we are part of. Research has evidenced that taking a 30-minute walk in nature everyday can help in reducing stress, anxiety and depression. Breathe that air. Still that mind. An ultimate sensory experience, an opportunity to connect with our senses of touch, sight, sound and smell.

Bare foot walking is also a great practice and aids the sense of connection to the Earth in addition to numerous other benefits which I invite you to research.

Gaze at the sky and be reminded to zoom out of your life and any difficulties and see the greatness and expansiveness of everything. I like to watch the clouds, seeing shapes and messages and watching the stars, making a wish upon the shooting ones. Not to mention the sunsets and sunrises; colour changing art masterpieces, where the practice of sungazing can be explored (only at sunset and sunrise, please research if you want to try).

Natures Plant and Master Medicines

Cultures around the world have engaged with natural remedies as healing tools and this traces back to ancient times. These medicines support dealing with the root cause of the problem, healing this, to allow for true good health and wellbeing to take place. Western society has gone so deep into pharmaceuticals that our ancient and effective medicines and remedies are often forgotten and neglected.

A reason for this is linked to people having very busy lifestyles and needing a quick fix (pill) as opposed to taking a herbal tea twice a day for a month, for example. Another reason is that many people are unaware of these options, as it is not taught as mainstream knowledge. To have knowledge of herbs and their properties could support our society to focus on daily prevention, rather than waiting to need a cure.

If you feel drawn to natural medicines, find someone experienced in what you are interested in, and importantly who has a good heart with good intentions. For herbs and remedies, speak with a herbalist. For Chinese medicine, a Doctor of Chinese medicine.

Master medicines are referring to sacred medicines which come from plants and animals on Earth, to support profound healing. Mother Earth provides all the medicines we need to support our physical, emotional, mental and spiritual selves.

Cultures such as those in central and south America have kept sacred plant medicine and master medicine ceremonies alive, sharing their wisdom and holding space for those who wish to go into the darkest depths of themselves, address challenges head on, express and release all emotions trapped inside, have insights into their actions and life purpose and expand in love and strength.

Many of these ceremonies work with psychedelic natural medicines to connect closer to spirit- spirit around us and within us. Our core essence. They are beautiful teachers and reminders that this life is just but one chapter of our soul's existence, and prompts us to remember the bigger picture. In doing so this supports us to be kinder, more peaceful, less judgemental, more expansive, more free. They help us to work and recognise the shadow parts within ourselves, the areas we need to develop in order to continuing striving towards being the best version of ourselves.

Spiritual master medicine ceremonies are profound and must be treated with respect and only engaged with in a sacred ceremony format, not recreationally. These master teachers have a spirit and must be acknowledged and respected. For sacred spiritual master medicine ceremonies, a trusted practitioner and compassionate space holder is essential (beware of those on an ego-trip).

It is important to prepare for this journey, not only physically reducing toxins (following relevant dieta's e.g. no alcohol, no synthetic drugs (first two very important to be out the system for a few weeks), no meat, no sugar etc) but also preparing the mind and soul.

This can be done through consistent meditation (most important), written reflections, time in nature, and other spiritual practices. This should ideally be done for a few months prior to engaging with the medicine. The medicines teach us a lot, but it is down to the individual to put the lesson into practice and apply it to daily life, which takes commitment and consistency.

The more work you put in to yourself prior to the ceremony, the more stable, safe and expansive your experience will be. This also prepares you with the mindset of continued consistency of self-improvement and self-love, to continue applying this to your life post ceremony too. The more you put in, the more you get out. Then what you learn, you put into practice.

Do not approach this option as a 'quick fix'- not doing the preparation work, rushing into it and expecting life changing events may happen, but you may be disappointed, triggered and have perhaps a less desirable or even traumatic experience. It is also important to consider any health implications and existing medications before engaging in any such ceremony.

When truly respected, prepared for and facilitated well, such ceremonies can change lives. They can eradicate depression. They can support life meaning. They can support healthier lifestyles of no longer having desire for toxins such as alcohol and synthetic drugs. I have met someone who took cocaine for 40 years, who did one ceremony and has not touched anything since.

The experience is different for everyone. Only seek it if you feel the internal calling and trust your gut regarding the time, place and people who will be part of this journey with you. From my heart to your heart. AHO.

11. Food: Gratitude, Mindfulness, Ayurveda, Alkaline

Food is our medicine. Something we regularly take from our external into our internal. It plays a big part in how we think, feel and act. We need to be mindful of what we eat, how natural it is and how different food items make our body feel.

Also, feeling gratitude and taking a moment within to give thanks for this food to nourish us, appreciating the gift that is before us. We can hold our hands above our food and send this grateful loving and nourishing energy into the food, intending it to make us feel good and give us energy. GAME CHANGER! We can do this with water too. This energy affects the food molecules itself and impacts how the food affects us. If we are the cook, we must ensure to cook with love and good intention, as that is what will go into the food.

A few times in my life I have turned to Ayurveda. Ayurveda originates from India and goes hand in hand with yoga practice. Part of Ayurveda is addressing the foods we eat in addition to health treatments, daily practices and lifestyle. The healing principles are to support balance of the three Dosha's (Elements- fire (Pita), air (Vata), Water/Earth (Kapha) in the body. This practice explores different body types, as food which is good for one person may be bad to another. I worked with an Ayurvedic practitioner who read my pulse, looked at my tongue and gave me a personalised plan. I explored this when I was 21 and it had excellent effects on my digestion. I was vegan at the time and was struggling to get all my necessary nutrients and this approach to food and lifestyle really helped me regain balance.

The second dietary awareness for me was learning about alkaline diet and how we need foods that support our bodies to be in their natural alkaline state. When we have too much acidity, it can cause numerous health problems such as indigestion and inflammation which can lead into serious disease and illness.

Everyone's body is different, but for the majority, processed foods, sugar, alcohol and processed meat and dairy can cause acidity in the body. You don't need to be perfect, but it is good to be aware of these factors. Eating fresh and local is also something to strive for where possible.

12. Morning Drinks

How we hydrate and start our day is important as after sleep is when our body needs to restock on fluid and minerals. In the mornings, I like to have all, or some, of the drinks below and I feel great when I am doing this.

- A pint of warm water- to hydrate, kick start the digestive fire (that's why it's warm) and flush the system

- Alkaline: Have a pint of warm water with added:
  - ★ Lime or lemon squeezed
  - ★ Celtic sea salt (pinch)
  - ★ Cayenne pepper (pinch)

- Alkaline smoothie: Blend and filter/ juice:
  - ★ 2 x green granny smith apples
  - ★ 1 x large leafy cabbage leaf
  - ★ Big chunk of ginger
  - ★ Juice of lemon or lime
  - ★ Water

  Optional extras for green juice:
  - ★ Coriander/ parsley (helps to detox heavy metals out of the body)
  - ★ Dandelion leaves (helps cleanse the kidneys- make sure to drink plenty of water throughout the day to flush them through)
  - ★ Sea moss (contains most of the minerals our body needs)
  - ★ Camu Camu powder (great form of vitamin C)

13. Bach Flower Remedies

Bach flower remedies were developed by Dr Bach in the 1920's. They are 38 natural remedies to address the array of emotional and mental imbalances humans can experience.

The essences are derived from natures plants and trees in England and each address a specific imbalance. For example, it is said that 'Pine' helps decrease Guilt, 'Larch' to build confidence, 'Star of Bethlehem' helps recover from trauma and grief, 'Wild oat' helps for uncertainty of correct path in life.

The most well-known one is 'rescue remedy' which is a combination of 5 of the Bach flowers and is used to help reduce anxiety. It includes Cherry plum (mental breakdown), Rock water (terror), Star of Bethlehem (grief or trauma), Impatiens (impatience) and Clematis (dreamy state).

Bach flowers are super powerful when taken consistently and the right dose. They have helped me a lot. They can be found online or in natural health food shops. I recommend consulting with a Bach flower practitioner or reading a Bach flower remedy book to increase your own understanding.

14. Positive Affirmations

I know positive affirmations can feel awkward initially, but to persevere through that and embrace genuinely this practice, can have powerful effects on re-wiring our brain and changing the energy we have and give out. It impacts our view of self, which then impacts how we show up in the world and who we are.

Thoughts such as: "I am positive. I am kind. I am strong. I am courageous. I am generous. I am compassionate. I am intelligent. I am worthy. I am beautiful. I am a great human being. Today is an amazing day. Thank you" can have interesting and powerful effects.

Think these thoughts as often as you can and would like. Watch the film 'Inside out 2' for a good visual explanation of how our 'Sense of self' is developed.

In the summer of 2023, I had an intense physical and mental health crisis. The scariest time of my life. I realised for my physical body to heal, I first needed to calm and re-order my mind, to attract the energy of healing. I started writing pages (5 x A4) of affirmations which I would read to myself every day without fail. This had a profound affect and helped me immensely. Read the book 'You can heal your life' by Louise Hay to support with this.

A great song I love which has a similar message is called "Positive" by Macka B and can be found on YouTube. A great song to get ready to in the morning to start the day. You could even learn the words and then sing it to yourself in the mirror.

15. Oracle Cards/ Positive Affirmation Cards
These can be positive and uplifting and a nice part of morning or evening routine to feel good and get a message for the day or guidance. Meditate, be open, connect and then trust the message that comes through for you. My favourite cards are the 'Spirit animal' and 'Angels and Ancestors'

16. Gratitude
Gratitude really is the right attitude. You can do this in many ways. One way I like is training myself to have three thoughts and feelings of pure gratitude when I first wake up and right before I sleep. This will amplify energy, improve outlook and will bring more positivity and synchronicities our way.

More formally, we can have a gratitude journal to affirm the practice more deeply and experience, what can be, more profound and expansive effects. A book which helped me on my gratitude journey at age 20, is called 'The Secret' by Rhonda Byrne, which I fully recommend. A following book she wrote called 'The magic' also contains great daily practices you can try over numerous consecutive days and serves as a great guide.

17. Writing

I love writing and it is a very helpful tool for me. I like writing poems, journals, gratitude diaries, plans, to do lists, dreams and experiences. It is an important medicine for my healing and allows me to go deep into the darkness, face it, experience it in its totality and then, from that point, re-find the light.

To express ourselves and allow our thoughts to be expressed on paper and flow freely is so empowering. We often have the answer and the solution, so allowing our thought process to play out can lead to our clarity.

There may be an emotion tracker app you may prefer to writing. App examples are: Mood Meter, Daylio, Moodtracking diary.

18. Connecting with the Moon

Connecting with the moon and aligning with its stages, either taking action or inaction. Turning inward or expressing outward. Time in the light and time in the dark. In balance. You could engage in full moon and new moon ceremonies alone or in a group to bring more awareness and focus to these cycles.

New moons are times to set intentions and begin to plant seeds for the month (moon cycle) ahead.

A full moon is time to admire and appreciate all the gifts life has given, all progress made on new moon intentions.

The ceremony could be simple and involve candles, writing goals/ reflections, meditation, prayers, affirmations, yoga, fires, singing, oracle cards etc. It is also a good and nice time to connect with the medicine of the Cacao, to help with opening the heart and feeling connected to Mother Earth.

For women, also look at the moon and at which point of the moons phases your bleed comes. Where this is can tell us about where we are at and what our focus is at this time in our life.

New moon is the 'white moon cycle', ready to focus on family and loved ones.

'Pink moon cycle' is when the moon is waxing towards full and it represents you opening and coming into your power.

'Red moon cycle' is to bleed with the full moon and indicates the medicine woman- in a stage of service to the community and planet, sharing our gifts for the benefit of others.

The 'purple moon cycle' is when the moon is waning back to new and represents time to go inwards, to reflect, rest, work on our internal world. All stages are important, and we often transition between them.

In a nutshell that is my understanding of it, and I invite you to explore further. To get into your natural rhythm of bleeding with the moon cycle you cannot be taking the contraceptive pill of other hormone birth control. These do not allow your body to sync with the moon in its natural rhythm and can lead to many health problems and imbalances within the body. The bleed is a sacred time for women and should be honoured and respected, not shunned. We need to learn to develop a positive connection with our bleed, feeling the relief present when it comes and releasing what no longer serves us. Be gentle with yourself during your bleed, rest for 1-2 days as much as is possible, connect with your body. Our intuition and psychic abilities are also amplified during this time, so it is a great moment for meditation, Qi Gong and other spiritual practices. Men, you can support women by supporting this process, allowing time and space and by understanding which phase of the moon she bleeds with.

19. Cacao

Cacao is a heart opening, loving and grounding plant medicine. She helps us to feel that deep connection with Mother Earth, opening our hearts like a mother's love. Cacao helps us to clear our mind and gain clarity, connect with our intuition and she helps heal and expand our sacral chakra, our centre for creation, to create and weave our own magic into this life.

Cacao is a sacred medicine plant that has been an important part of communities in Meso-American cultures for over 4000 years. Cacao was known as 'The food of the Gods'.

With intention, connecting with Cacao is a ceremony and has been used in spiritual, ritual and shamanic ways for thousands of years by Meso-American communities. The Aztecs also used dried cacao beans as a form of currency and at one time they were thought to be more valuable than gold.

Cacao also has many health benefits- containing high magnesium and iron content for relaxing muscles and helping the body to release tension- Theobromine dilates the blood vessels increasing blood flow throughout the entire body; to the brain and to the heart by up to 30-40%. The fresh oxygenated blood is full of antioxidants and essential vitamins and minerals, energising muscles and clearing brain fog.

So, Cacao can be both a relaxant and a stimulant. It will depend on intention, quality and quantity of what you are drinking in addition to the present state of the person. As always, everyone is different so always listen to your bodies response and what feels right for you. Check for any health contraindications you may have and be sure to buy ethically and sustainably sourced cacao, where you can trace it to its source and support those communities.

20. Ecstatic Dance Movement Medicine

Movement as medicine, flowing, dancing, becoming the bass, the flute, the piano. For me, attending ecstatic dance allowed me to experience a sober rave, with spiritual connection and the freedom to move and dance to the music without fear of judgement. Ecstatic dance is basically that- a sober or conscious rave, often began with meditation, connecting the group and at times Cacao is consumed before the dance to open the heart and provide energy. The music takes you on a journey, starting slow, increasing in tempo and intensity and then ending slow. The aim is to allow your body to move to the music in any way you want, without judgement. The body knows what movements it needs to help release tension and clear blockages. You may shake, spin, jump, hop, roll, twerk, dance in any style you want and on occasion I have seen a man spend much of the dance in a head stand against the wall. This practice is a space where you do not need alcohol or drugs to give you the confidence to let loose and really explore your body's moves.

Ecstatic dance workshops often take place at spiritual festivals and in cities. Look on Instagram tags and social media to find what is near you. It is a wonderful way to discover the confidence to express yourself among others. You can apply the same concept attending your favourite raves too! I love drum and bass and at Mr Traumatik I was one of the last ravers still going, no alcohol or drugs and the most hyped! The music and movement are the medicine.

21. Connecting with Instruments and Making Sounds

This is a great way to express oneself. A passion, a profession or a fun exploration. Music can accompany ceremonies, festivities and occasions. The music we listen to impacts us so be aware what lyrics you are singing along to and affirming in your life.

Music can take us on a journey within or it can be our expression in the world. Learning to use our voice to make a variety of sounds and noises is a profound exploration. I did this during ceremonies and workshops with Tlilik Tekuani and wow it feels good to make this vibration within. This is another technique to clear our energy channels, through the vibration of sound.

Tlilik Tekuani discovered different sounds to connect to Earth ("Aaayyyyyy"), Sky ("Eeeeeee"), expansion within ("Ooohhhh"), gathering creative energy in sacral (Ooooooo) and to expand and share that energy with the world ("Ahhhhhhh").

Sometimes a good scream into a pillow can help too. Never bottle these energies inside. Always release, and sound is a fantastic way to do this.

22. Birth Charts

As mentioned at the beginning of this book, I invite you to explore your birth chart for your current character and being that you are in this present life. This will help you and others to understand you and show you how to work with your strengths and challenges. You can search for free astrological birth charts online and just need to provide your location, date, and time of birth. Prepare to be mind blown!

Remember though, your soul is infinite and goes beyond this definition. Just see this as your instruction manual for this lifetime. Also remember there are many versions: Western astrology birth charts, Mayan Calendar, Chinese signs, Human design, Ayurveda etc. Choose which ever you are drawn to, or explore them all!

23. Self-Care

Engaging in self-care in all of its forms is the most important thing to create time and space for. Take a shower, a nap, time to write, to talk kindly to yourself, watch a movie, have a hot chocolate, a herbal tea, eat fruit and vegetables, drink water, give yourself a hug and tell yourself how much you love and appreciate the very special you. Run a 'goddess' bath for yourself with rose petals, candles, essential oils. Give nutrient rich nourishing food to your body. Stretch, sing, dance, express. Rest, recuperate, hibernate. Massage your own feet with essential oils. Have a movie day. Meet your own needs, whatever they may be in the moment. Listen to all the subtle messages your body gives you.

Remember that self-care is not selfish, the more we can fill our own cup, the more abundance we have to overflow to others, impacting those around us positively. If our cup is already empty, what we can give to those we love is not sustainable. We must strive to be autonomous in meeting our own wellbeing as best we can. We have the power and the biggest impact. Also accepting to be open and receive help coming our way. Life is all about giving and receiving, in continuous flow. Remember people love to give, so do not feel bad asking for help when you need it, allowing someone to help you could actually make their day, increasing their own sense of fulfilment and wellbeing.

24. Finding your Passion

Finding the activity or thing which empowers us, gives us energy and makes us feel alive is a treasure of life. Our passion is what helps to give our lives zest, enjoyment and meaning. You may already be aware of your passions or if this is still unclear this opens the doorway to the opportunity to try a variety of activities and subjects!

Only through trying something a few times will you know. This could be surfing, cooking, helping people, playing an instrument, dancing, nature, computers and technology, sustainability, sports or anything! They may often can change and transform over time which is perfectly normal. Find your passions and engage in them often to keep occupational balance between your life engagement with self-care, productivity and leisure. The passion is the leisure but can often also be integrated with self-care and productivity (if for example you can earn money and a living through your passion).

25. Cleansing Energy and Space

This is how we can carry out spiritual hygiene- as we wash our physical body, our spiritual body needs washing too, to help cleanse and clear stagnant or heavy energies. This can be done using <u>sustainably sourced</u> aids such as white sage, sage, frankincense, Palo Santo, Copal, Lavender or others.

Combine burning this, with prayers- first offering gratitude and giving thanks to Mother Earth, Father Sky, the Great Spirit, all ancestors and guides, spirit animals and guardians of the directions (N, E, S, W and guardians of the place you are in). Then request support in cleaning yourself and your space or the item or person of anything that does not serve their highest good. Using a feather, guide the smoke down to the Earth around your body/ what you are cleansing. Then ask for support to help the self/ person/ space to be filled with healing, positive, compassionate, and peaceful energies, or whatever feels right, and do the smoke around and down the body again with this intention.

Jim taught me to guide the smoke down as the smoke itself rises up which cleanses, but to smooth down with the feather helps to ground, so being balanced. Being ungrounded and only cleansed can leave a person less protected in their energy. Jim taught me using white sage. He explained to start with windows and doors closed so the whole room is full of the smoke around me. At the end, the doors are opened, and smoke guided/ wafted out completely. To be confident and assertive with the prayers and asking any dark energies to leave.

I use an abalone shell to put the sage in, representing water. The sage represents Earth. The fire and smoke once lit represents fire, and the feather represents air. Connecting with all of the elements. When the prayer and ceremony is complete. Close the space by once again offering thanks and smoke to Mother Earth, Father Sky, and all mentioned above. To complete the close say 'thank you AHO'. Take a few deep breaths in your lower dantian energy centre and meditate. Always release all the smoke from the room to open the windows and ask energies to go to the light or back to where they came from. Say with confidence and kindness.

26. Cold Showers/ Cold Water

Having cold showers daily can have many positive benefits. It aids the body to train itself to deal with stress, helps circulation and blood flow and boosts the immune system to name a few. I first came across this when a friend showed me a documentary about Wim Hof, AKA the Iceman. I encourage you to check out his work and try for yourself. Even just 30 seconds of cold shower at the end of your normal shower is better than not doing it at all. Wild swimming in cold waters is great to experience, but always go with someone and have hot drinks, warm clothes and hot water bottle for after and ensure to get changed quickly. Be mindful ladies if on your bleed, cold water exposure is not always recommended at this time.

Also check the water is safe to swim in.

27. Giving back to Community and Earth

Acts of service for people and planet is beneficial for all involved. Smile at strangers, complete a litter pick, take a sustainable straw and spoon with you to avoid unnecessary plastic use, join a community project while travelling, help that person carry their bags, give fruits and water to those in need. Good deeds every day help us feel good and can uplift and inspire those around us.

28. Pay it Forwards

A film I found inspiring in my youth is called "Pay It Forward." Its core message is about doing a meaningful good deed for three strangers and asking them to pass on the kindness by helping three more people. This idea aims to create a ripple effect of positive actions, encouraging everyone to embrace this generous mindset.

29. Yuka App

This app I came across in 2024 and it is very insightful. With it you can scan barcodes of products and have an honest report about what it contains, highlighting things which contain substances hazardous to our health. This can be done for food and beauty products. I had never been that aware of what I was putting on my skin or washing my hair with, however our skin is our biggest organ and most porous, absorbing all toxins we cover it in, which then our system has to deal with. This app is helpful in identifying this in products so we can make an informed choice.

Many of these products are not thought to have hazardous amounts within that one product (hence why they get past regulations), however, take into consideration that an average woman getting ready in the morning may easily use 10-15 of these products, leading to toxic overload (shower products, lotions, make up items, deodorant, perfume etc).

30. Qi Gong Sensory Massage

There exists an Autism intervention called Qi Gong sensory massage which aims to deblock and open up/ regulate the senses through touch which stimulates blood flow to different areas of the body. More information can be found on this from the book called: 'Qi Gong Massage For your child with Autism' by Louisa Silva. This book teaches how to do the massage and the explanation behind each movement. This technique stems from China and has been proven effective particularly for children under 12 years of age, by numerous credible research studies, which show improvements in sensory and emotional regulation, communication, sleep, digestion and learning after 5 months of daily massage.

The massage is taught to be given every day by the caregiver/ primary caregivers as part of evening routine and takes about 15-20 minutes.

I have just qualified as the first person in England to be trained in this massage and I am excited to empower parents and carers with this intervention.

Thank you for reading.

On the next page feel free to draw and create your own 'Self-care toolkit' of all the things that make you feel healthy, strong, positive, joyful, and peaceful and things you are interested to try.

Blessings to you for this life and all your soul's journey.

From my heart to your heart,

AHO.

_____'s

self care toolkit

Self-Care Toolkit Checklist

	Practice	Tried?	Notes
1	Meditation		
2	Morning and evening breathing		
3	Deep breathing		
4	Breathwork		
5	Qi Gong		
6	Bamboo Sticks		
7	Martial arts/ Exercise/Yoga		
8	Acupressure mat		
9	The Body Scan		
10	Nature		
11	Ayurveda/ Alkaline foods		
12	Morning drinks		
13	Bach Flower Remedies		
14	Positive affirmations		

15	Oracle cards		
16	Gratitude		
17	Writing		
18	Connecting with the Moon		
19	Cacao		
20	Ecstatic Dance		
21	Instruments and sounds		
22	Birth charts		
23	Self-Care		
24	Finding your passion		
25	Cold Showers		
26	Cleansing your space and your energy		
27	Giving back to community and Earth		
28	Pay it forwards		
29	Yuka App		
30	Qi Gong Massage		

Be present, joyful, loving and free.

Be more Kody.

***

Printed in Great Britain
by Amazon